Christian writer, Lynn Baber, shares her wealth of experience and passionate love of Jesus Christ in her books, in person, and in the round pen working with troubled horses. She learned the principles of worthy leadership and right relationship from decades as a successful equine professional, in business, and by the work of the Holy Spirit. The truth of faith that overcomes fear is the same for both Christians and horses.

# AMAZING GRAYS, AMAZING GRACE

# READER COMMENTS:

"There are so many books in the world, and so little time to give even good books the time they deserve. There are some books, that as you read them, they are so rich, so full of imagery and truth, that you take your time trying to absorb every nuance and make your own connections. *Tess of D'Ubervilles* by Thomas Hardy and specifically two of C.S. Lewis' books (*4 Loves* and *Mere Christianity*) hold a special place in my heart as these kind of books.

I can add Lynn Baber's book, *Amazing Grays*, to that particular book shelf. - Melinda F., *Boots and Saddles*


Using common sense peppered with anecdotes from her horse training experience, Lynn Baber gently leads the reader to the clear connection between life as we choose to live it and God's grace. The chapters [of *Amazing Grays*] are stand-alone inspirational reading and practical equine advice, from relationship to leadership, success to failure, and discipline to distractions. - Carol Upton, .reviewer


*Amazing Grays, Amazing Grace* is a wonderful departure from the myriad of horse books that are available on the current market. ... Convicting yet inspiring, [it] encourages the reader to pursue excellence in relationship to both the horse and (more importantly) to the Lord Jesus. - Jill


I have given *Amazing Grays* to people of various backgrounds, including folks with no inclination to the horse world at all, such as business executives, craftsmen/women, YMCA staff, neighbors and friends. I also share this "extremely relative to today's world" book at Cowgirl Chapel services as well as to members of my home "Fellowship of Christian Cowgirls" group. - Claudia W.

Lynn Baber's new book, *Rapture and Revelation*, has not been written for the reader who wishes to have his or her ears tickled. There are plenty of Christian books and e-books catering for that, but not this one. It is a book-study offering simple truth about the times we're living in, but it's also a challenging book, leaving no room for the reader to express anything but "yes" or "no" for their answers and decisions. No room for fence-sitters! - Roger Williams, Australian radio broadcaster and blogger

*He Came Looking for Me* is a book like none other I have read. The author's unique writing style is both captivating and refreshing. Baber masterfully parallels the experience of seeking and restoring foals once sold in the breeding program, to the heart of God that comes looking for those needing hope and redemption. I read it a second time in one sitting and found myself reading parts out loud to friends. You will find inspiration in the pages of this easy to read, but hard to put down book. - David M.

*He Came Looking for Me* is an extraordinary book that should be a must read for animal lovers. The author beautifully correlates the story of reuniting with two lost horses with the promise that God makes that He will never lose us. ... She never allows us to forget that God has a plan, and that all God asks us to do is simply move one foot forward toward that plan each day. ... Truly a wonderful book that I cannot wait to pass on to the animal lovers in my life. - Jen S.

# AMAZING GRAYS, AMAZING GRACE

Pursuing relationship with God, horses, and one another

Lynn M. Baber

ISBN # - 978-1-938836-03-9

Published by Ark Press

Amazing Grays Ministry.
PO Box 187
Weatherford, TX 76086

# AUTHOR'S NOTE

Many of the greatest lessons and blessings in my life are a result of horse training - me training horses and horses training me. There are few concepts found in the Bible that don't make wonderful illustrations for establishing a right relationship and worthy leadership with horses. Horses are far more honest and consistent study partners than other folks.

Over the years I developed a particular love of stallions. Communication with horses (especially stallions) is direct, clear, consistent, and short. I tend to write the way I talk, so if I ever have the privilege of meeting you in person, you should find the experience a familiar one.

Over the years, I was blessed with wonderful clients, students, and horses. Just as I hope each of them knows how grateful I am for the trust they placed in me, let me thank you as well, for taking the time to read *Amazing Grays, Amazing Grace*. Should you be disappointed in any way, the fault is mine and not with the Author of the message.

God bless your journey.


Lynn Baber

# TABLE OF CONTENTS

# INTRODUCTION

The day is unveiled as the morning sun slowly begins to rise above the black-green trees and deep purple hills, each new angle of sunlight creating an original canvas upon which God's artwork appears to those who are awake to behold its glory. As dawn progresses, trees take on more distinct form, and the buildings and structures on the hills rise out of a flat landscape as if elevated from below.

Grass becomes a luxurious carpet of vibrant green as new sunlight reflects through droplets of morning dew. Vague forms of horses contentedly grazing become illuminated as the solar spotlight brings their once ghostly images into sharply focused view, allowing me to identify each one in turn. My eyes search for confirmation that my little herd has made it safely through another night. I see the tall, black mare, the powerful dun, and my two grays. All is well.

This is a day that the Lord has made; let us rejoice and be glad in it. God is ever faithful, each morning bringing new life and opportunity to His family. I rested well last night, safe in the assurance that though I slept, He was awake and watching over me. With dawn, the responsibility for my horses passes from God to me, and I will be faithful to them until night returns and I pass the watch back to heaven.

Have you noticed how birds seem to sing with special joy in springtime? Their music accompanies my study as I pause again to look through my east window to the horses grazing beyond, grateful for yet another opportunity to walk with the Lord. My greatest blessing is being a child of God, knowing that He loves me beyond my capacity to comprehend. How can humans possibly grasp the unknowable truths of a relationship with God and with our Savior, Jesus Christ? What could possibly bridge the distance between heaven and earth and allow mere mortals a glimpse of eternity? It is grace.

The Holy Spirit gives each of God's children a unique context that allows us to build a personal relationship with Him. For me, that context is horses. Twenty years training horses was my preparatory school, providing the key I needed to finally grasp what were previously only vague elements of my pursuit of relationship with God. The key to my relationship with God was provided by my amazing grays, Bo and Swizzle. I chose them, and they chose me. Working through my daily lessons with the Holy Spirit allows me to direct and deepen the bond I share with my grays, just as working with horses blesses me with a greater understanding of the absolute truth and promise of God's Word.

The secret of life is relationship with God. The important question is not how, why, where, or when; the important question is "Who?" This book is a collection of concepts and stories, an opportunity to learn how horses allow us to find closer relationships with God. Woven into the fabric of the message is love, correction, wonderment, obedience, accountability, success, failure, birth, and death. But the heartbeat that gives each life is a relationship with the Lord.

Are you pursuing a right relationship to God? As a child of God, *Amazing Grays, Amazing Grace* will help you learn to communicate with the Spirit and experience correction and trial as your habit of task slowly changes to a habit of obedience. As your training progresses, you will begin to see the possibilities of relationship with the Lord that were but ghostly images in a flat landscape. Prepare for the dawn and experience the blessing that a relationship with God brings to your other relationships. Learning to abandon to God will teach you how to be a better parent, teacher, friend, minister, leader, and horse owner.

God has chosen you to be his child.

*Praise be to the God and Father of our Lord Jesus Christ, who has blessed us in the heavenly realms with every spiritual blessing in Christ. For He chose us in Him before the creation of the world to be holy and blameless in his sight. In love He predestined us to be adopted as His sons through Jesus Christ, in accordance with his pleasure and will—to the praise of His glorious grace, which He has freely given us in the One He loves.*

*And you were also included in Christ when you heard the word of truth, the gospel of your salvation. Having believed, you were marked in Him with a seal, the promised Holy Spirit, who is a deposit guaranteeing our inheritance until the redemption of those who are God's possession—to the praise of His glory.*

Ephesians 1:3–6, 13–14

Amazing grace, how sweet is the sound of my grays as they snuffle contentedly in their stalls, secure in the knowledge that I watch over them as He watches over me.

*Lynn and Bo*

# THIS IS THE PROMISE

*If what you heard from the beginning abides in you, you also will abide in the Son and in the Father. This is the promise He has promised us—eternal life.*

1 John 2:24-25

*Endurance is not just the ability to bear a hard thing, but to turn it into glory.*

William Barclay (1907–1978)

The desire for freedom in Christ does not gradually develop over months, years, or a lifetime, although our discovery of it may be made either instantaneously or over a long period of time. All who were called from the beginning will discover this desire for freedom, but the *how* of discovery is as unique to each of us as our individual relationship is with the Father.

~ ~ ~

The day is calm as the wild horse quietly grazes in the valley washed with the soft sunlight veiled by gauzy clouds formed by the humidity in the atmosphere. For the moment all is quiet, still but for the movement of the wild horse slowly comparing one blade of grass with another and the occasional swish of his tail in response to a solitary fly. Nearby more wild horses graze contentedly while another small group naps in the shade of gnarled trees commonly found where homesteads were made and then overgrown in decades past. This land belongs once more to rabbits, quail, coyotes, and wild horses.

If we watch closely, we can see that the wild horse has stopped nibbling and stands motionless as if it were a videotaped image and we just pushed the pause button.

~ ~ ~

My senses pick up something that causes me to stop grazing. The faintest breeze is gently moving down the valley, trickling through the air like a tiny rivulet dancing on the long hairs of my muzzle. When I become aware of what my sensitive nose already noticed, I recognize *something* and lift my head from the grass. *What is it,* I wonder. I lift my head higher, close my eyes, and open my nostrils as wide as I can to gather in what the cool breeze is bringing to me.

My spirit recognized the scent of freedom before my brain was able to process it. *There is something there, wait...* Yes, there is something being carried on the breeze. I take one tentative step forward then hesitate; my flaring nostrils take in another deep draught of clear air and another—this is air like I have never breathed before. Without realizing it my feet had moved me forward again. I stopped. *Which direction is the breeze coming from?* What is the source of this scent that I recognize but can't identify? Lifting my head even higher, I slowly move it in a full arc from one side to the other, testing the air as I attempt to determine the origin of this tiny inviting scent.

I make one more complete sweep with my nose, tasting the air as I pass from left to right. *Yes, the scent is coming from beyond the hill where the sun begins its daily journey.* My hooves move forward with one hesitant step and then another. Each stride lengthens as I gain confidence that I am going in the right direction because the scent becomes the slightest bit stronger with each step. Soon I am lined out in a purposeful walk, following this most elementary scent, this scent of freedom. Now that I know what it is I must follow it until I reach my destination. I give no thought to how long the journey will take or what obstacles may have to be overcome. I only know that this scent promises freedom, and I must find the way.

Passing by the group of horses napping under the tree my only focus is the path ahead, keeping true to the scent of freedom so I will not lose my way. I do not notice when one of the other grazing horses slowly stopped nipping fresh green blades and lifted her head, testing the air and trying to identify what the breeze was bringing. Because I no longer see the horses sleeping under the tree I did not notice when the young stallion in the middle of the group woke, opened his eyes and flared his nostrils to deeply breathe the scent of the gentle breeze...

Though I don't know it yet, I will have company on my journey to the narrow gate standing open for me...

...and grace will lead me home.

# WILD HORSES AND THE
# NARROW GATE

*Enter by the narrow gate: for wide is the gate and broad is the way that leads to destruction, and there are many who go in by it. Because narrow is the gate and difficult is the way which leads to life and there are few who find it.*

Matthew 7:13–14

*Your own conduct and actions have brought this upon you. This is your punishment.*

Jeremiah 4:18, 22

*The prophecies of Jeremiah are a powerful and timely reminder that human beings are not pathetic babes in the woods, but mutinous people. We live in times of devastation, war and calamities, but those who know God have this consolation, that in and above all these calamities God is working out His purposes absolutely undistressed, and although clouds and darkness are around, they know that the clouds are but the dust of His feet.*

Oswald Chambers

It's a bad time in the world to be a wild horse. Man has severely limited the areas in which they may freely roam. With man in charge—and that "man" is the United

States Government—wild horses are dying of both starvation and thirst. Being a wild horse was a great life back when they were allowed to exist under the rule of God. As eventually happens when man's rational law takes over, a bell begins to ring ever so faintly. Over time the sound becomes progressively louder until even the deafest ear can hear its death knell.

Man is in charge of nearly everything today: which babies are born and which are not; who will die at the end of his natural life and who will not; how parents may raise and educate their children; and how the money you earn will be spent, even if it is spent in a way morally abhorrent to you. We are like wild horses today, living under the mutinous thumb of man's poor judgment. Thankfully, we who know Jesus Christ as Lord are assured of ultimately finding the gate that opens to the world God intended where we may escape the bondage of man's rule to live forever, freely roaming heaven's lush verdant pastures.

**The Scent of Freedom**

Jesus tells us that the gate to ultimate freedom is very narrow. Wild horses move by instinct toward that open gate. At times, the narrow, rocky trail will result in momentary hunger, thirst, thorn scratches, and bruised hooves, yet those that recognize the scent of freedom will persevere until such freedom is theirs.

Along the way are small oases of pasture and water. Wild horses who choose to linger in the ease of such moments will eventually find them overcrowded and be forced to fight one another for the few bits of grass and puddles of brackish water that remain.

The path leading to the narrow gate which opens to freedom and life eternal had been blocked, seemingly forever, by an earlier stampede that caused an avalanche of massive boulders to block the only way to freedom. . . horses have been searching for another way out for centuries but there is no other. What happened to open the pathway to the gate? Jesus Christ personally removed every boulder, stone, and pebble. Prior to the resurrection and ascension of Jesus Christ the narrow gate was closed and locked, permitting no access to the freedom beyond.

Jesus Christ opened the locked gate, entered heaven, and the gate remains open today. The instinct to search for the path to freedom is provided to some by the Spirit of God. Those wild horses that will not search out the way to freedom will live out their lives seeking food, water, rest, and the opportunity to procreate.

The Holy Spirit gives the scent of freedom to the horses chosen by God. As His wild horses near the gate the scent of freedom becomes stronger with each hoofbeat. Have you ever seen wild horses intent on getting somewhere? They don't look to the left or to the right. When they are in forward mode they don't look behind. The greater the scent of freedom in their flaring nostrils the more fixated on their goal they become, not caring that the path has become stonier and the thorn bushes closer to their heaving flanks. They press on until they are through the gate—to freedom.

Can one wild horse get another through the gate? No. A mare will offer her life for her foal unless panicked or resigned to the ultimate loss of the foal. A mare knows when her foal is too weak to keep up with the herd. She will stay with her baby as long as possible and then abandon it when her very life hangs in the balance. She will go forward with the herd so she will live to birth another foal next spring.

Under quiet, unhurried conditions, one horse may certainly attempt to coax his herd mate through a narrow path, rocky ravine, or roaring river. One horse will show the straggler the way and invite him to "follow the leader." The invitation is only extended so many times. If the leader is following the scent of freedom, eventually he'll abandon the unwilling horse. If the lead horse has no compelling scent of freedom, he may choose to return to his companion and they will live or die together.

Herd behavior begins to change when wild horses find their circumstances becoming more and more difficult. When food and water become scarce dominant horses begin to kick away those further down the pecking order. God planned for the strong to survive so when times of plenty return the strong will have mated with each other so the herd may continue.

## Selecting a Mate

Humans used to choose mates in a manner somewhat similar to horses. Mares select the stallion they believe has the best genetics to produce vigorous foals. Women used to select husbands who were able to provide food, shelter, education, and guidance to produce strong children able to help support and continue the family.

Horses, unlike men, weren't given the concept of self. Horses do not have the capacity to consider God's plan and then reject it. Men have this option and have wildly exercised it to their detriment as both the family of man and as children of God. The entire concept of reproductive freedom is that any woman (or man) has the right to make any choice they please in producing offspring with the support and endorsement of society and the government. This is idiotic on its face. Horses are so much smarter than we are in this respect. Nearly every other mammalian society exhibits greater wisdom than man when it comes to procreation.

Man breeds weakness into his society, and this trend is increasing at an alarming rate. God gave us a plan for procreation that worked well until man decided he had a better idea. As a society, we have evaluated God's plan for procreation and rejected it in favor of self-gratification. William Penn wrote in *Fruits of Solitude* that "Men are generally more careful of the Breed of their Horse and Dogs than of their Children."

Can a mare raise a foal on her own? No. Mares don't conceive unless they actually meet a stallion and become carnally acquainted. God's plan doesn't include test-tube stuff. Artificial insemination and embryo transfer are used in selective equine breeding because man just can't keep his hands out of the action. The result indicates we're doing a poor job indeed considering the state of horse markets since 2008.

Once carrying a foal a wild mare stays with the band of mares collected by the herd stallion. Wild mares need the stallion for protection and the herd for safety. Did you know that mares usually eat before the stallion when food is in limited supply? This is God's way to preserve the health of the developing foals.

A mare on her own will not get pregnant, and if pregnant and the stallion and herd is lost, the chance of her own survival, much less that of the foal, is slim to none. But, one may ask, don't wild horses just keep mating even when times are tough? Not so much as you might think. If a mare doesn't have sufficient body condition, she will not cycle well and may not even allow a stallion near her. Even if she does mate, she will probably not conceive. If she should conceive, the embryo may be absorbed or aborted. God's plan has no error.

A similar situation applies to humans. Women with insufficient body fat may fail to cycle normally and be unable to conceive. This is a natural form of birth control. Without sufficient food for the mother to stay healthy there is obviously not enough for a baby. In the instance where a woman chooses to maintain ridiculously low levels of fat in her body due to extreme exercise commitments, she may be too dedicated to her sport to be a great mother. She, however, has the option to change her circumstance, unlike a wild mare.

Creating human embryos in a laboratory introduces weakness to our "herd." One example where the wisdom of wild horses exceeds that of humans is Octomom, Nadya Doud-Suleman Gutierez, who managed through six pregnancies to birth fourteen children via in-vitro fertilization with no father and no visible means of support. This wouldn't happen in any mammalian society operating under God's plan.

In similar circumstances, wild horses would be faced with the sad necessity of leaving a herd member behind to perish who couldn't keep up. But then, horses aren't nearly so foolish as to get into such a fix to begin with. Most of our great societal issues and conundrums are the result of man deciding his plan was better than God's. The result is usually chaos and heartbreak.

Wild horses feed themselves because God provides the food. Wild horses work up to sixteen hours every day finding the right mixture of available food to stay healthy. Wild horses exercise, they play, and older horses companionably gather to watch as young ones frolic about.

Wild horses protect one another. They have a nearly perfect system of justice. Wild horses are obedient to God.

God gives some of the wild horses the scent of freedom. The gate to freedom is narrow. Few will enter. Most will get caught up along the way satisfying temporary urges to graze, drink, or play, or be otherwise distracted in a dozen different ways. God cleared and marked the path to freedom for those He had chosen. Disobedience caused the avalanche that blocked the path. God sent His Son to clear the path of immovable boulders and to open the locked gate. The gate remains open, so the wild horses may pass through to the freedom beyond.

Are you content to linger in the ease of the moment, or will you persevere until you reach the gate that Jesus left open for you? Do you recognize the scent of freedom?

# WISDOM AND INSTRUCTION

*The fear of the Lord is the beginning of knowledge, but fools despise wisdom and instruction.*

Proverbs 1:7

*The wise man will seek to acquire the best possible knowledge about events, but always without becoming dependent on this knowledge. To recognize the significant in the factual is wisdom.*

Dietrich Bonhoeffer

Proverbs 1:7 speaks to the need for foundation and learning. *Amazing Grays, Amazing Grace* is filled with references to building foundation and the process of learning. Indeed, each day that passes without adding knowledge is a day wasted. The proverbial reference to the fear of the Lord is a clue that unless we walk with wisdom, the manner in which we live our lives may have dangerous ramifications upon the outcome of our lives. When are we most likely to seek out wisdom and instruction? It is when the task or circumstance we face is potentially most dangerous.

Would a prudent man seek instruction before driving an Indy car at two hundred miles per hour? Would it be wise to fly a fighter jet by just winging it, without instruction? Would you attempt to defuse a bomb without prior experience or education? Would you fight a two-thousand-pound bull with nothing more than a cloth cape for preparation? Would you attempt to rope and ride a one-thousand-pound wild mustang without instruction?

The answer to all of these questions is obviously no. Why? Because the probable outcomes are so patently disastrous that only fools would make the attempt. Yet, some fools do.

There are idiots out there who would be thrilled to strap themselves into an Indy car without instruction and gleefully push the gas pedal through the floor. Thankfully, no Indy car owner would let such a person anywhere near his or her car. Not only would the car be wrecked, but in all likelihood the car owner could expect to be sued by the driver's survivors and possibly lose everything he or she owns. This being the case, foolish people can't easily get their hands on a real Indy car.

But I bet there is a video game that simulates Indy car racing. Once the fool begins to perform well with the video game, he may really begin to believe he can drive the real thing. Why? Any common sense of fear the fool may have had has been replaced with the belief that his performance on the video game adequately judges his skill level, opening the door to a potentially dangerous situation. After all, the fool rationalizes, "I exhibited pretty good skills in simulation and should now be successful driving a real racecar."

Would the U.S. military turn over a fighter jet to someone with no flying experience or pilot training at all? Of course not. Most people aren't idiots and have enough wisdom to never conceive of such foolish enterprises. Yet, there is probably a video game out there that might remove God-given fear from a foolish one who confuses pretend with reality. Perhaps there is even a video game opportunity for want-to-be bullfighters.

While some may argue that all the video games mentioned in these illustrations could be considered instructive, most, to my mind, would be more accurately described as destructive. Now, let's look at one example I can speak to personally: riding a wild mustang. I've done it more than once.

## Riding Wild Mustangs

What happens when one tries to capture and ride a half-ton package of terrified bone, sinew, and muscle without wisdom or instruction? Bad things happen. Usually the horse suffers the most. Would I have any sympathy for the inexperienced fool who is severely injured should he try to rope and ride one? Not much. I would, however, feel desperately sad for the poor mustang.

Horses captured in the lonely places of the western United States are living textbooks of how to successfully be a wild horse. Whether a young horse or an adult, the very fact that they survive in harsh conditions prove they have both the skill and temperament wild horses need to stay alive. A lion is not a housecat, and a wild horse is not a domestic horse. Lions have developed relationships with humans and wild horses can make reliable mounts. However, not all lions make pets and not all mustangs are suited to be little Jenny's 4-H project.

One of my customers brought me a four-year-old mustang mare for training. The mare was really bad about having her feet handled and had never been saddled. Once the mare and I developed a relationship she made the commitment and become a willing student. Within just a few months she went home to her family and became a trustworthy mount for a rider with limited skills and was calm for the farrier to trim. This previously wild mare was completely suited to relationship with a human.

Another customer introduced me to a different kind of wild horse when she brought him to me for training. A relatively young mustang gelding, this fellow was cute but didn't seem to understand how to relate to a human at all. He wasn't overly aggressive, but I sure needed to establish a beginning. The first day I worked with him I was able to pet him and have him stand quietly to be haltered. He learned that the best place in the world was standing patiently next to me.

Many times in my training career I earned the entire month's wages the first day. This was one of those times. That first day of training was long, but we got where we needed to go. Or so I thought.

On the second morning, I went out to his pen to halter and groom him before moving on in the training process. His reaction to me entering his pen was not one whit different than it had been the day before. That mustang ran around as if I was a mountain lion looking for breakfast. It took a refresher course to get him to relax and agree to play. Within thirty minutes he was haltered, groomed, and ready to proceed.

Since there are a few more things I'd like to share with you, I am going to cut to the chase on this story. I rode that mustang. We walked, jogged, and loped. We backed, side-passed, and rode out into the desert. But each and every morning he looked at me like I was a hungry mountain lion. We could make only so much progress in each day's lesson because I had to work through each and every bit of his training each and every day.

There are lots of good mustangs out there. Unfortunately, this horse had proven his success at being wild and should have been left out there in the mountains. I tried to get my customer to cut her losses, but she really wanted to save this wild horse. That was, until he bucked her off. I could work through all the stages on each ride but she couldn't and there was no way this horse would ever be a trustworthy partner for her. Unlike that other mustang mare, this one was just destined to be a wild horse. He could be ridden, sure—but would he ever remember that fact from one day to the next?

Can one safely race an Indy car? Fly a fighter plane? Defuse a bomb? Does the bull ever lose? Can wild mustangs make good saddle horses?

Yes, to all of the above. But in what circumstances might one hope for success? First, there must be sufficient respect (fear) for the consequences of failure before attempting any of the challenges suggested in these examples. This respect, or fear, leads the wise person to seek out instruction. Which comes first, the chicken or the egg? Which comes first, the wisdom to seek instruction or instruction that creates wisdom?

Neither. What comes first is fear, or respect, for the car, the plane, the bull, the horse. The question of practicing prudence when contemplating an obviously life-threatening task is not very controversial. We expect Indy car drivers to be experienced, fighter pilots to have successfully acquired the requisite instruction, and horse trainers to be qualified. Most rational folks would agree, but not all. Mind you, there are plenty of fools out there who would argue that they are exceptions to the rule.

**Choose Wisdom**

It is easy for reasonable people to reach consensus about the mortal dangers inherent in flying fighter jets, diffusing bombs, and bull fighting. Could we also all agree on the concept that life itself includes mortal danger? Who would argue the point that all who live will ultimately die?

There would be some I am sure, but as Ron White, a Texas comedian, tells his audience, "You can't fix stupid."

How many people actively seek knowledge and wisdom about something as simple as just living their lives? Life itself is an inherently dangerous pursuit. All men die. What then?

Learning to train horses, build foundations and eventually relationships, is a lifelong pursuit. No one will ever completely master the horse. No driver will ever totally master the racecar. No fighter pilot will ever master the possibilities of waging war behind a cockpit windshield. Every horse is an individual and changing racetrack conditions and the actions of the other drivers create new puzzles for Indy car drivers with each successive lap. The weather and enemy combatants present an ever-changing battlefield for the pilot-warrior.

The only opportunity to make it from life to life, and not life to death, is through the never-ending pursuit of relationship with God. The landscape of our lives changes daily, creating new challenges. This seeking after God requires us to develop wisdom, through knowledge of Him, to be able to evaluate our constantly changing conditions and react with prudence.

*Every prudent man acts with knowledge, but a fool lays open his folly.*

Proverbs 13:16

How true. Think about the ever-expanding line-up of reality television shows from *Jackass* to *Survivor*. Not only do foolish people believe they are exceptions to the rules for the somewhat sane, but they are willing to make their case on national television and bet their lives in the process. There are foolish people in every organization, family, church, and community. They simply will not acknowledge their need for instruction and training. But no one ever knows it all. Why do you think Olympic champions who just won several gold medals still have coaches?

If you are not an experienced horse trainer get instruction and develop wisdom before jumping on a wild horse. If not for your own sake, for the sake of your family and the innocent horse you might injure or kill. Don't try to race or wage aerial war without the proper dedication to gaining life-saving knowledge. Don't take a gamble on how your life will end without the necessary knowledge and foundation that will lead you to right relationship with God.

Are you a seeker who hopes there is a place prepared for you in heaven? Are you willing to bet your life on it? The Holy Spirit is ready to begin your lessons. Experience and knowledge are yours for the asking. Today is a good day to begin. And, unlike that wild mustang gelding, I hope you retain all you learn from one day to the next.

Let us seek wisdom and knowledge together.

# YOU MUST HAVE A HORSE TO TRAIN A HORSE

*Watch out for false prophets... By their fruit you will know them.*

Matthew 7:15-16

*The greatest obstruction to the working of God comes from those who give themselves to interpreting the words of God rather than doing them.*

Oswald Chambers

How many avid horse people search out books and articles about horse training? A bunch. I warn folks to be on the lookout for these two kinds of people, anyone who tells you he knows all there is to know about horses and anyone who says he completely understands the book of Revelation. If you should meet one of these people, *run!* Neither is true, nor is either even possible. Anyone who believes he knows all there is to know about horses or Revelation is either woefully misguided or a false teacher. Don't listen to or read another word from his lips or pen.

The impact of Facebook, MySpace, Twitter, and similar social media has created the perception in many, many people that the world anxiously awaits their next opinion blog. Our collective sense of self-importance soared off the chart a number of years back. Indeed, when I

~ 37 ~

heard that then fifteen-year-old Miley Cyrus was going to write her autobiography, I thought, *She's barely through puberty. What great wisdom could she possibly have to share?*

This potential for instant celebrity has only exacerbated our natural human desire to pontificate and expound upon important or popular subjects. In essence, this is evidence of our innate laziness and egotism. We believe our personal insights into both Scripture and horse training to be brilliant. Social media allow us to share our thoughts and opinions without the work of crafting sentences and paragraphs, using applicable illustrations, or crediting sources.

The topics of horses and religion always attract large listening or reading audiences because no human has ever cornered the market on them. You can read about wonderful relationships that others have with the Lord or with their horse. We see evidence of such amazing relationships on television, in the movies, in print, and on the Net. Evidence of these marvelous and rare relationships may seem to border on the miraculous. Stories abound of miracle dogs and miracle horses. Just enter either of these phrases in your favorite search engine, and the number of hits will astonish you. I did that today and came up with 48,300,000 hits for "miracle dog" and 28,100,000 for "miracle horse." Just on Amazon.com alone there were 789 results for "miracle horse."

**Miracle Relationships**

Are there truly miracle animals? Personally, I don't think so. The vast majority of the stories of miracle animals could be more accurately described as miracle relationships. Miracle relationships are both passionate and personal. The dog that is so identified with its owner that it is able to give advance warning of seizures is evidence of the power and depth of their relationship, not evidence that the dog is itself miraculous. This proven ability to predict seizures is not readily transferable from one person to another. That dog might be more easily and quickly trained to react similarly for another human, but not without first establishing some supporting relationship with the new person.

Do some of these stories truly share miracles? Perhaps. But even if you are able to find a case where an astonishing act was performed by a dog or horse in the absence of a relationship with the human involved (there's nearly always a human involved), the act would be an act of God, not that of a miracle animal. There was a recent story about a yellow Labrador retriever whose canine companion was hit by a car. The yellow lab took hold of his friend and pulled him off the road and out of heavy traffic. Is he a miracle dog? No. The story is evidence of a very special relationship between the two dogs.

Let's consider police dogs, the K-9 units. The relationship between the handler and dog is critical to the effectiveness of the dog/officer partnership. There are many moving stories of heroism and mercy that K-9 units brought to an emergency situation. Police dogs live at the home of their human partners as an integral and beloved member of the family. If relationship weren't the key to success officers would simply pick up a dog at the station's kennel prior to each shift.

**Relationship Is Required**

The amazing relationships a seeing-eye dog has with its blind owner; the police dog has with the officer; or the bond a miniature horse has with her owner that allows her to be a service animal, are not built by reading books or watching videos. In every instance, the human must be properly paired with an animal and a relationship established. The depth of relationship defines the ultimate level of service an animal will perform for a human. Sometimes no training is needed apart from a close and loving bond. You cannot build relationship unless you are in a relationship. You cannot learn to train a horse without first having a horse.

Little benefit is realized if you read the Bible with no relationship to the God of the Bible. There is little benefit to anyone who pays attention to folks who comment on biblical or horse training issues who offers nothing more than an intellectual position. It is impossible to expound on Scripture in any meaningful way without a relationship with God. Those who share insights and commentary about training horses must have a relationship with a horse. This is the minimal requirement. Once this is established you may begin to evaluate the benefit of their opinion.

Have you participated in any equine competition at a relatively high level? If so, did you simply gather up the reins for your first ride on a new horse and win? Probably not. Equine competition is based on teamwork. One of the reasons we keep at it is because no one has ever mastered the possibilities of the horse-human partnership. To compete on horseback is to combine two separate physical bodies and two separate personalities and then throw emotion on top just to make it interesting. You may have an off day when your horse feels fantastic. You may be on top of your game on a day your horse is just out of sorts.

All horse-and-rider successes are built upon a framework of leader and follower. Most horse and rider teams need time to learn each other's personalities, forge effective methods of communication and correction, and, by doing so, develop trust and confidence in their mutual ability to succeed—not just for you, the rider, or your horse as a trained athlete, but confidence in the ability of the team. Usually the rider becomes the leader and the horse partner the follower. There are, however, some instances where the horse is the leader, the tutor, and the rider is the follower, the student.

Some horses learn their jobs so specifically that regardless of who is sitting in the saddle and how correct or incorrect the rider's input might be, the team is successful. These horses have great self-confidence and perform to a high degree from a habit of task rather than a habit of obedience. There is some mixture of the two, but if you doubt which habit provides the greatest influence, leap up into that saddle and ask such a horse to perform outside its usual range of maneuvers. Chances are the horse will do as it always does and not what you ask. A perfect example of a horse with a solid habit of task is the rental trail horse. These horses follow the one in front of them no matter who or what is on their back. But trying to get one to deviate from its routine is next to impossible and the stable owner won't appreciate your attempts to untrain his horse.

Two types of horses are the most difficult to ride: those that are hardly trained and those that are highly trained. The barely trained horse has little ability to either give or receive effective communication, and the highly trained horse is acutely responsive to tiny, sometimes imperceptible, cues. Two ounces of excess pressure on a highly tuned horse may result in a big, completely unexpected response. Two ounces of added pressure on the barely trained horse will probably get you no response at all.

## Why Should You Listen to Me?

Beware of people who read the Bible and offer everyone a declaration of what the words mean or should mean. That person may have never lived or experienced what he or she speaks about with such certainty. The Bible tells us not to teach others how to solve problems that we have not first lived and conquered in our own lives. Folks who read a lot about the nature of the horse and how to train one may express their views and opinions with absolute certainty and with a certain air of authority. But have they successfully proven their theories in the dust of the round pen or replicated their results with other horses if, indeed, they were successful with one?

So, you rightly inquire, "Are you, Lynn Baber, different from such people? Why should we read your words or consider them potentially valuable?" Before I answer your question let me first make this statement: I do not know all there is to know about horses, nor will I attempt to explain the book of Revelation in any meaningful way.

Now that I have cleared that hurdle, allow me to make my case for your review and consideration. Indeed, I both applaud and encourage any reluctance to buy into my views without first asking about my credentials.

I have had the privilege of receiving instruction over the years from dozens of horsemen and horsewomen and hundreds of horses. I learned valuable lessons from gifted riders as well as from incompetent ones. I learned from outstanding horses as well as the few rogues I had in training. Although the basics of psychology generalize to the majority of humans, one must be careful to note that there are mentally and emotionally unstable individuals to whom normal rules and expectations just don't apply. The same is true of horses.

The skills and abilities that I learned over twenty years apply to most horses. But some horses are mentally or emotionally unbalanced. It doesn't matter if they were made that way by nature or circumstance; only a seasoned professional should ever attempt to work with them. Some may be rehabilitated and become useful or trustworthy horses. Many will not. Over the years I worked with some seriously unbalanced horses. Some became manageable, but only with strictly enforced routines and constant maintenance. Others learned but did not retain their instruction, remaining unpredictable and potentially dangerous if their routine varied even slightly.

One of the qualities or skills the good trainer must cultivate is the ability to separate sane, balanced horses from those who are not. Many times the observable behaviors of the normal and the abnormal horse look largely the same to the average horse trainer or owner. The good trainer uses previous successes and failures to discern which is normal and which is not by comparing the behavior to the specific circumstances. What caused the horse's reaction? Any single stimulus or pressure will yield a normal range of responses in most horses. If a particular horse responds way outside that range, the good trainer will note the aberrant reaction and keep testing to determine what situation he or she is actually facing. Both normal and abnormal horses run, buck, and kick. In what circumstances the horses choose to do so helps to establish if it is responding within normal limits or not.

Not only have I proven my leadership ability to build right relationships with horses, but I have done so with a variety of horses with great diversity of temperament, ability, and intelligence. If required, I am prepared to back up my words with action. As a horse leader I can prove in the physical arena what I offer in the intellectual arena.

## Trust, but Verify

What about my illustrations or comparisons relative to our relationship with God? I do not ask you to, nor would I want you to, accept my views as truth on their own merit. Read what I offer, consider it in light of all else that you know intuitively or rationally. Do the concepts I present ring true to you? Do they add to or help explain facts or experiences you already have? As a horse trainer I hope to provide you with information or concepts you haven't explored before. As a Christian, I hope to use life with horses to help illuminate your study of Scripture as revealed by the Holy Spirit. In the same way Oswald Chambers speaks to me and makes my relationship with Jesus Christ easier to understand on a human level, it would be a great privilege to be of similar service in a small way for you.

The relationship we work for with our horses is a lifelong pursuit. We will never master all that can potentially be. Our work will never be finished unless we lose interest and quit. It is easier for me to process questions about my relationship with God if I can restate the issue into trainer-horse terms. All becomes much simpler and I am able to gain greater perspective.

Whenever you hear or read statements about God and how to be rightly related to Him, you must always go back to the Word to verify the accuracy of what you heard. Do the same with what I write. Discover truth by going to your Bible and to the Lord in prayer.

## Authenticity

Many horse trainers teach one way to train to their students but can be observed using different and sometimes opposite methods with their own horses. If you encounter this situation find out if there is a reasonable explanation for the disparity. If not, find a different trainer to emulate. All too often similar situations may exist in other areas of your life—with preachers, teachers, politicians, and experts of many types. Is your preacher living as he preaches? If not, find another. Does the politician live by the words he or she so eloquently speaks in public? Probably not. Let's vote him out of office and find another more deserving and trustworthy. Does your physician constantly harass you about your weight and smoking? Is he a physically fit, trim, non-smoker? If your experts aren't great examples of what they preach to others, find other experts.

*. Search me, O God, and know my heart; Try me, and know my anxieties; And see if there is any wicked way in me, And lead me in the way everlasting*

Psalm 139:23–24

My desire is to be searched by God and found absolutely authentic and to live according to every word I write. My personal habit is to speak as if every word might be printed on the front page of a newspaper. If I would not want it printed, I try not to speak it. If there is any place where my words and behavior differ, I want to know so I can either clarify my words or correct my behavior. I want to truly be the leader my horses believe me to be. More importantly, I want to be the child God has called me to be.

The only way to learn how to fish is to fish. The only way to build great relationships is to devote regular time and significant energy to them -- and be in their company! You cannot be in a right relationship with God if you only hear His Word from the pulpit on Sunday morning. You will never build an amazing relationship with a horse if you spend each day indoors reading a how-to book or watching a training video while your horse is out in the pasture alone.

Theodore Roosevelt said,

*It is not the critic who counts; nor the man who points out how the doer of deeds could have done them better. The credit belongs to the man who is actually in the arena...who strives valiantly; who errs and comes short again and again...who at the best, knows in the end the triumph of high achievement, and who, at the worst, if he fails, at least fails while daring greatly so that his place will never be with those timid souls who know neither victory or defeat.*

God expects us to be authentic and consistent. Use this same standard when selecting your teachers. You must have a horse to train a horse. Look for teachers who have been in the arena, who have tried time and time again, who have persevered through failure and defeat until they reached a place of success and are willing to share their journey with you.

If you never come in after a day's work with manure on your boots, dirt in your nose, or sweat on your hatband, you are not a horse trainer. If you have never been stricken to the depth of your soul with the guilt of knowing that God sent His only Son to die for you, the Holy Spirit has never taken you to the woodshed. A shower will clean you up after a day in the round pen, but only the blood of Christ can clean you up from the inside out.

# IN THE BEGINNING

*In the beginning God created the heavens and the earth.*

Genesis 1:1

*Look one step upward, and secure that step.*

Unknown

The day begins as I enter the round pen already occupied by a two-year-old slick coated gray gelding sporting a long mane and shining tail. To begin our "dance" I watch the gelding to see how he reacts to me. Is he curious? Will he calmly look me over and watch my movements? Or will this gray youngster be fearful, quickly trying to move away from me, searching for any way out of this trap? The first step in training, in relationship building, is to observe the horse's response to me. Is he confident or fearful, aloof or panicked? Will he run from me or try to run me over?

The next few minutes are spent moving around the pen. I make frequent stops to look out over a nearby pasture; check out the wispy clouds passing overhead; bend quickly down to pick a weed growing in the sand—really doing anything other than acknowledge that the horse who shares the pen with me exists. All the while this charade is going on I watch "Gray" out of the corner of my eye to gauge his reactions to my movements. At this stage, horses will usually do one of two things; get more curious about what that odd human is doing or maintain a constant distance, moving away when their space is invaded. Today, Gray started by giving me lots of space, then he gradually stopped moving and began to quietly watch me. Good.

Once I know it is safe to turn my back on Gray it is time to begin establishing communication. This handsome gray gelding has not been haltered before and I know that walking directly up to him, slipping a halter on his head, and patting his beautiful neck is not an option yet. There is no way to build a relationship without a method of communication. The only way I have to establish any kind of a dialogue with Gray is through the application and removal of pressure. I have to establish this cornerstone of foundation before moving on. Body language is the language of horses. Gray doesn't know my language so I have to use his if we are to establish a beginning.

My first challenge is to ask a very simple question and then apply pressure until Gray gives the correct answer. Horses learn when pressure is removed, not when it is applied. Timing is everything. The first lesson I want to teach Gray is that pressure is removed when he gives me his attention. The right answer will be when Gray turns his head and looks at me with his full face. As a trainer, you must be precise in knowing what response you want in order to precisely reward it. I specifically want Gray to turn and look at me so I can see both of his eyes at the same time. The instant Gray gives the right answer all pressure must cease.

Gray is standing about thirty feet away, half looking at me. As I begin to walk toward him, he turns away. When only fifteen feet separate us, he begins to walk away from me. I stop. Gray turns to look at me. I can only see one of his eyes. I begin walking toward him again. Gray looks away and takes another few steps. I stop again. Gray turns his head just enough that I can see both his eyes. In that second, I turn around and walk quietly away from him. I remove the pressure. After ignoring Gray for maybe ten seconds, I turn to him again and start walking toward his side.

This time I get within ten feet of him before he starts to walk away. I stop. He stops, shifts slightly, and then continues walking away from me. I increase the intention in my step as I resume my deliberate walk toward him. As Gray moves around the perimeter of the round pen, I walk a smaller circle about ten feet off his side, following him as he goes. Before we've made a full circle, he stops, nervously twitching his ears, and leaves the ear closest to me steadily turned in my direction. I stop. He stops. I back up a step or two, now focused on his head. Gray turns as if to follow my backward motion. I can see both his eyes. I turn and walk away.

As I walk away, Gray turns his whole body so he is in the perfect position to walk directly to me. He stays focused on me. I look at the clouds again for a few seconds and then turn and take three steps toward the gray gelding. He does not raise his head higher, his eyes stay on me, and his feet don't move. I stop and turn away from Gray again. After a quick count to ten, I turn halfway back to Gray and begin walking to his left.

Big brown eyes follow me for a few steps until I lose his attention when he puts his nose to the ground and sniffs the sand. The moment Gray loses his focus on me I must increase the pressure until I have him back again.

When his eyes broke from me I moved closer to his body, still walking a loose arc around him. I focus my attention on his hip, almost trying to push the air into his hindquarters to move it away as I get closer. Gray notices I am not in front of him any longer and turns to look at me. As he turns his head his hip moves away from me. The moment I see both of his eyes I turn and walk directly away from him again. Gray takes two steps in my direction, then stops, continuing to watch me with his eyes.

Gray and I have had our first meaningful conversation. When he learned that he had the power to make the pressure applied by my positional challenge go away, and that the right answer was to turn and quietly face me, we established a beginning.

When I work with a horse for the first time the question I ask depends on the circumstances. Where, when, why, and how much pressure I apply are variables that change by the second. One very simple question is, "Will you move one foot backwards?" When one hoof moves away I remove all pressure because the horse gave the right answer. Another very simple introductory question might be, "Will you move your body to the left?" The moment the horse's nose tracks to the left and feet follow all pressure is removed. The first time a horse gives me the right answer we have established a beginning.

~ ~ ~

When we first yield to God, when we receive the first blush of faith in Jesus Christ as Lord, we establish a beginning. For both horse and human, the orderly process of training begins. The first steps are small, easy ones. Lessons become more complex as new skills and concepts build upon those already learned. The foundation of relationship begins to take shape—lesson by lesson, concept by concept. As is true with a worthy trainer and a horse, God is never done training His children. There will always be a higher order lesson to learn and apply.

Obedient and amazing horses are not made quickly, but methodically as the trainer teaches the horse more vocabulary, establishes greater trust, and both displays and creates more confidence and commitment. Obedient and amazing Christians likewise are not created instantly. God provides the perfect teacher, the Holy Spirit, to tutor us, quiz us, challenge us, and help us become the people God intends for us to be. The amazing and beautiful thing is how we can benefit and enjoy this relationship every day, at every step. Success is not a destination; it is the character and manner in which you live your life day by day by day.

Could God instantaneously create a perfect Christian? Sure. But that wasn't His intent when He gave man his nature. There is one standout example of a nearly complete transformation; when Saul became Paul. There hasn't been a repeat since, so we'll just have to accept our relationship with God as one we make stronger with each lesson mastered and as each day becomes the next.

Can the learning process with a horse be smooth and pleasant? Absolutely. I've always told folks that training a horse is fairly boring to watch when properly done. The training process only gets exciting (and potentially dangerous) if the trainer has not properly prepared the horse for the lesson. Every new lesson should so naturally follow the previous one that the horse has only to make a small change to succeed and attain a new level of skill. Steps are small, and the circumstance of the pressure being applied to the horse is such that his most natural physical response is the one we want. I believe the best trainers are the ones who know the most ways to accomplish the same result with a horse. If one trainer knows four ways to teach a horse to side-pass and another knows six ways, the latter is probably the better trainer. Horses are every bit as peculiar and individual in the ways they learn as people. What works with one horse will not succeed with another. Each trainer–horse relationship is unique.

Why do our lessons from God get so messy and, at times, downright painful? Could it be because we do not properly prepare ourselves and insist on pursuing the wrong behavior? God will never give us a free pass when we don't make the correct response to His request. He will apply incrementally more and more pressure until we "give." Pain is usually the result of our outright refusal; pain is never the object of a lesson from God.

**Psychic Shock**

There are only three instances where I will punish a horse physically. Should a horse bite, strike, or kick at me––no matter the situation––I will respond immediately and powerfully and in a way I hope the horse will remember. The idea is to take three seconds and apply psychic shock, making the horse believe he is in mortal danger. Once three seconds have passed I consider the matter closed—no grudge——and move on as if the bad behavior never happened. As far as the horse is concerned all is forgiven, but in reality I pay closer attention to his body language so neither of us get injured. Hopefully the horse will think twice before acting out the next time.

Whether the offender is a young foal who doesn't know better or a mature horse spoiled by some human who taught it to bite, I never let a serious infraction pass if I have control of the horse and plan any future with it. When a half-ton horse bites, strikes, or kicks, there is always a real possibility of severe injury or worse. In the few circumstances where a horse exhibited rude behavior toward me and I did not have control over it, I pretended not to notice its attempt to show me who was boss. Hey, if I don't see it, I have no obligation to correct it.

We have had one or two recipient mares (mares carrying foals for other mares) that were rude to me without my making any big deal out of it. These mares would only be on my ranch until they weaned the foals they carried before returning to the reproductive clinic that supplied them. They weren't considered part of my herd and I was careful to separate them from my other horses. We did have a couple of really great recipient mares, Sarah and Hilda. They were treated like family and when it was time to return them we made sure they went into programs that were very selective about their mares, where Sarah and Hilda would be valued as individuals. These girls had earned the right to a great life and we did our best to accommodate them when they left us.

The horses we didn't claim, we didn't correct. If you find yourself being trained and corrected by God, consider yourself blessed with this proof of His love.

# PROPER DISCIPLINE

*We do not know what we should pray for as we ought ... but He who searches the hearts knows what the mind of the Spirit is, because He makes intercession for the saints according to the will of God.*

Romans 8:26-27

*Grace and indulgence are not synonymous.*

Unknown

What should you do when a horse kicks, bites, or strikes at you? This is a situation where there must be a Plan B in place before Plan A is launched. As the trainer, the leader, I must understand my "followers." Over the years I have developed enough experience with horses to have a pretty good idea of what each will do in any given situation, or at least I am able to compile a very short list of how each horse might possibly react. Many times when I work with a horse I know the next move he will make before he does. Sometimes you have to think several steps in advance, taking the horse's next probable reaction into consideration before making a move. It's kind of like playing chess.

Horse trainers must know what their next action is before the horse reacts to the previous one. I control the pressure and stressors on the horse in training. Each horse has a limited number of possible responses to any cue. The horse may move left, right, forward, backward, sideways, up or down. Knowing where a horse is likely to move its foot during a lesson is important when determining where I should put mine. Horses weigh far too much to have them dance on my toes—again. It's happened a time or two. I'm only human, but I have learned from my mistakes.

## When a Foal Misbehaves

When I work with a foal I need to pre-plan for our mutual safety and know what reaction I will use should the foal grossly misbehave. In a herd, mares other than the mother of a bad little actor will correct the offender when it transgresses. Great mares teach their own foals respect for their mamas as well as how to play nice with herd mates. When a mare corrects a foal she may shove it with her head, nip it on the rear, give a loud squeal, or apply a non-lethal kick or push. I simply do the same. I don't remember ever biting a foal, but I've sure done the rest.

Every year we always seemed to have one or two little darlins' that were too big for their britches. Every foal is born understanding the methods I use to correct bad baby behavior. When bad baby behavior isn't fixed you are guaranteed to get bad big horse behavior later.

When a foal's infraction was a big one, I sometimes squealed loudly while immediately (pre-planned) pitching my hip into the baby's ribcage or shoulder. My preferred target is the foal's hip. The hip has greater muscle mass than any other body part and is generally a safe place to smack a foal—but you have to be really good at evaluating body position and knowing in a split second how the foal is likely to respond so you don't get kicked. Safety first. Don't try this at home!

There are many ways to discipline a horse. Punishment is used when there is a real danger of injury. Even with the wide range of philosophies surrounding the subject of disciplining children, it is pretty much agreed upon that sure, swift, meaningful punishment should be attached to behaviors that may result in serious injury. When you see your toddler reaching his tender little hand out to the gas flame on your stovetop, you care very little about using a measured tone of voice. You yell and grab the kid!

Immediately following the rescue, you very sternly and emphatically state, "Never, never, never do that again! Do you understand?" Your actual intent is to scare the child nearly to death and make a big enough impression to last the rest of his life —psychic shock. Your response will be very similar if you see that same little blessing's sister running out into the street as a speeding car approaches. Save the kid first, then scare the heck out of her so she lives to give you grandchildren.

## Be Prepared

Punishing a horse uses the same logic. Dangerous offenses demand big responses. What if the horse in question is an adult stallion and not a foal? The principle remains the same although the response will look different. I have been known to squeal at studs who also understand and respect the tone and demeanor of an angry mare. When dealing with adult horses, and especially stallions, the pre-planning part is of even greater importance.

My safety is in greater peril when a 1000- to 1500-pound hairy mass of testosterone decides to act out. Preparation is key. Every interaction and lesson must be well thought out in advance. Before doing anything I must be about 90 percent sure I can accomplish my goal when applying pressure to that stallion so he will choose to yield to me. Even with this preparation there is still a 10 percent window for disaster left on the table.

I set the plan for handling that remaining 10 percent before starting the lesson. The number one rule I have for stallions is that they get no wiggle room at all on toeing the line of proper behavior. No breaks. No gimmees. Stallions must be absolutely behaved at all times or there will be a consequence. Mares and gelding are allowed a little leeway at times. I used to tell my stallions that yes, life was unfair, but the upside was they got the chance to procreate. Perhaps they considered it a reasonable trade off.

For insight on what planning is required when training horses, and especially stallions, read Luke 14:28-31. Jesus tells us no experienced builder builds or king wages war without the means to finish or win. Our lesson is to consider the end of the process and what is required to complete the process before we begin the process.

After a few years as a trainer I was drawn to stallions. I really enjoyed them and had many stallions in training, frequently having more stallions in the barn than geldings or mares. Stallions are easy to figure out. Stallions know their purpose. Stallions are usually direct, literal, and can make excellent students. Mares are subject to hormonal changes and are not always consistent in their responses. For years, I found geldings less interesting than stallions, but now I put geldings at the top of my list of preferred horses to train. The three differences between now and then are: I have no breeding program, I no longer train other people's horses, and my interest is in building relationships. Having a stallion only makes sense if you intend to breed him.

It is absolutely true that within every good stallion there is probably a great gelding. Many veterinarians consider castration an emergency procedure; it must be done before the owner changes his mind! From the horse's perspective, it is far better in most cases to be a gelding than a stallion. Stallions tend to be abused more than mares and geldings due to lack of understanding on the human side of the equation. Unless allowed to breed mares there is really no upside to being a stallion. This is a particular soapbox of mine, but I will refrain from any further elaboration. Suffice it to say that 99.9 percent of all male horses should be geldings.

And not all horse trainers are good stallion trainers. Every good stallion trainer is not a good mare trainer. Horses have personalities and physical limitations based on gender just like people do. Generally speaking, you cannot push an eighteen-year-old, 80-pound female gymnast to the same physical or emotional level you can an eighteen-year-old, 220-pound male football player. Testosterone plays a significant role in muscle and bone density as well as psychological makeup.

**Stallions Are Different**

During my years showing halter horses I showed lots of stallions. When I was first starting out I was challenged, since most judges did not like women leading stallions into the show pen. Twenty years ago there were only two or three women in the country who had enough shank power to show halter stallions. My use of the term *shank power* here is not in the political sense but in the sense that only these few women had demonstrated that they possessed the psychological makeup necessary to convince a mature stallion that he was beneath her in herd pecking order. These women could convince a stallion to cede a leadership position to them. At first, I thought such discrimination was simply unfair, but I was determined to be successful showing stallions.

A few years later, after I become a judge, I learned to share the opinion that most women shouldn't lead stallions into the show pen. Imagine my surprise. This realization provided me with insight into a number of other issues dealing with women in what were traditionally male roles. For now, however, I'll stay on track and limit the discussion to stallions. Most women are not made to mentally dominate a stallion. This isn't a judgment and it isn't a criticism. It is simply a fact.

When women lead stallions into the show ring the horses often try to sneak in a tiny little rude behavior just to see what will happen. These little acts of disrespect often went largely unnoticed by most of the ladies on the end of the lead shanks. The majority of the lady exhibitors had no idea that the stallions were giving them what I call "the pony finger." I expect you understand what I mean. If not, e-mail me and I will explain. These situations usually happened when the regular trainer showed the stallion in the Open class and the woman showed in the Non-pro or Amateur class. The stallion knew perfectly well how to behave, but when the trainer wasn't in the arena the stallion decided to test the leadership of the woman with the lead shank. When his first little wisecrack went uncorrected, the stallion saw an opening for making a little bigger "mistake."

The usual drill was that the woman didn't, or couldn't, correct the stallion in a meaningful way, and he escalated his bad behavior until the class was over or someone intervened to maintain safety. At one horse show a young stallion reared up and raked a front shoe right down the lady's face. Why did he do it? Because he could. Such behavior isn't necessarily the result of meanness; it's just a stud being a stud when left to his own devices. I don't know how many times I kept an eagle eye on an exhibitor having little turf battles with the stallion she was showing, trying to determine the exact moment when I would have to either grab the lead shank myself or send the ring steward over to prevent catastrophe.

In December of 1996 I showed a long-yearling quarter horse stallion in halter at the Arizona Livestock Nationals. At the proper time I led him into the arena to walk toward the judge and then trot away so the judge could evaluate the colt's quality of movement and soundness. After that, class procedure is to squarely set up each horse in a single line (head to tail) for the judge to evaluate and mouth (check their bite). This particular stud colt was one of the sweetest guys I'd ever had in the barn though not one of the smartest. He was just a really good-looking, kind sort of colt. I didn't use a lip chain on him, which was routine at the time. He had never offered to misbehave—until I asked him to trot away from the judge that day.

Unexpectedly he reared up and waved at the crowd, knocking my cowboy hat into the dirt. Even though the young stallion was really only playing, his hooves had come pretty near my face. In that split second I saw the judge quickly turn his back to me and I proceeded to run that colt's behind backwards with "great collection." The judge knew that correction needed to be fast and definitive. He turned around so he didn't have to notice the brief discussion I needed to have with the young stallion. After a short delay I calmly walked my colt over to line up as usual. He won the class. In fact, we took Reserve Grand Champion that day.

There are many ways to discipline a stallion. We'll just leave it at that. Working with stallions is not something you should ever attempt by just reading up on the subject, so I'm not going to take the chance of giving anybody any ideas here.

Here we are, back at the beginning. The first stage of building a meaningful relationship is communication. Once we establish a way to communicate we begin to build vocabulary. Simple lessons become concepts. There is no substitute for consistent, regular interaction. Every time we are in the company of another, whether horse or human, we are either offering something new or reinforcing a point already made. As a good horse trainer or good parent, we are responsible for properly preparing lessons and to conduct safe, confidence-building lesson experiences.

Is there an optimal time to begin training a horse? It is far easier on both horse and trainer to begin the process as early as possible. If the relationship bond is created early, the dance will be far less dusty and the degree of pressure and correction far less than when training starts later. This is true of both horses and children.

Retraining adult horses or mature humans is more difficult and requires a much higher skill level, far greater patience, exposes both student and teacher to greater danger, and the possibility of success is not as high as with early, correct training. When you have to retrain or work with a mature stallion or adult man, there is greater natural resistance to overcome. You may have to remove existing habits, skills, and methods of survival that these individuals relied on for years in order to replace them with new ones. Old survival skills are replaced through right relationship to the leader. The concept of obedience has to be taught clearly, fairly, consistently, and safely. The only other possibility is pure dominance, which is another subject entirely and dealt with later in this book.

# UNABLE OR UNWILLING?

*Nevertheless not My will, but Yours, be done.*

Luke 22:42

*I must not forget to thank the difficult horses, who made my life miserable, but who were better teachers than the well-behaved school horses who raised no problems.*

Alois Podhaisky

Whenever our horse, child, spouse, or employee does not do as we request, there are only two possible reasons to explain their behavior: they are either unable to respond as we ask or they are unwilling to respond as we ask. As the responsible party, we must be able to distinguish between these two conditions and make a response appropriate to the situation. Action is always required. No response is nearly always the wrong response.

Enforcement, or punishment, will never fix inability—and no amount of education will ever fix unwillingness.

The art of leadership is determining which situation you are dealing with: one who is unable or one who is unwilling. As the leader, once the root cause is established, you must provide whatever is needed to make the follower able or provide whatever motivation will lead them to willingness.

What about the issue of communication? It does not change the process. The leader must decide whether adequate communication was given. If it was, then the follower is using lack of communication as an excuse. This is one example of unwillingness. If the leader determines that communication was not sufficient, then the follower was unable. If you as the leader are not sure which is the true condition, always give the horse or the other person the benefit of your doubt.

I have trained several horses over the years that gave me incorrect responses on purpose, trying to convince me that I had over-cued them. There are some really smart horses out there, believe me. Usually the problem was one of boredom; the horse wasn't challenged enough in my lesson plan and was looking for new entertainment. The horse was also testing my leadership.

When a horse (or child) is unwilling to comply, we must apply an appropriate consequence each and every time. Education is not the fix many activists and politicians would have you believe. It is not true that "knowledge is virtue"; the belief that if only one knew the facts, one's behavior would fall right in line with prevailing ideals of right and wrong. Education never creates willingness. Education can only address inability. The devil himself believes in God - he is fully aware of the facts. Yet this true knowledge does not incline Satan to obedience to God because he is absolutely unwilling.

Virtue standing alone is priggishness. Knowledge standing alone has no application and no value, but is an example of paralysis of analysis. God has a lesson plan for us. Have you already achieved the first stage in a meaningful relationship with Him? Have you established a method of communication? Do you make yourself available to His instruction in a consistent, regular manner?

Are you learning to be obedient? When He asks something of you, are you able to comply? Are you willing to comply?

God knows all there is to know about how to apply pressure and how to get our attention. I assure you He is well able to handle any tantrums we throw and will have an appropriate consequence ready each and every time one is necessary. We are born knowing that God exists. We are born with the language He uses to speak to us and His timing is always perfect.

Jesus Christ is the good shepherd, the best trainer. How lucky you are if He calls you one of His own. Whatever He calls you to do He will enable you to do. You have only to be willing.

Once communication is established, we have a beginning.

# BO AND SWIZZLE

*For where your treasure is, there your heart will be also.*

Matthew 6:21

*I heard a neigh, Oh, such a brisk and melodious neigh it was. My very heart leaped with the sound.*

Nathaniel Hawthorne

Could I be a more fortunate person? As I write these words, I am blessed to look out my window and admire four beautiful horses grazing contentedly in a large pasture that only sports this particularly perfect shade of vibrant green during the spring in north central Texas. On the far side of the pasture is eight-year-old Asti, a tall, elegant black quarter horse mare with a long mane, a tail that drapes across the top of the grass, brilliant white socks, and a full blaze. Her right eye is the most beautiful shade of cornflower blue. Asti always looks like she is dressed for a formal event and stands nearly a full hand taller than the two geldings and nearly two hands taller than the smaller filly. Not far from elegant Asti is my husband's gelding Copper, trying out one fresh green blade of grass after another. Tender, sweet new grass is a special delicacy for horses used to the dry, tough graze left behind by winter.

Technically, Copper is a dun quarter horse, his shiny copper-colored coat gleaming like a newly minted penny in the sun. Copper is best described as buckskin, his coat set off by a thick black mane and tail, plenty of dun factor and black "points." Copper is built like a brick you-know-what and is an intriguing mixture of both refinement and massive muscle with just a little Disney cuteness thrown in that many are drawn to.

Six-year-old Copper will forever be the pesky little brother of the herd although he is the second eldest. Watching him work his way into the personal space of elegant Asti is fascinating entertainment. How does Copper get away with his frequent little acts of blatant disrespect? Well, he doesn't always, as the occasional nicks and dings from hooves and teeth in his beautiful coat reflect. The ladies are not always amused by Copper's antics, yet he returns to annoy them time after time. To be honest, he is making progress on redefining the social rules of the herd. I will continue to watch, laugh, and learn.

Enjoying center stage in the pasture are Bo and Swizzle, my amazing grays. Why do I think they are amazing? Because I would never have expected these two gray horses to be the ones I ended up with after twenty years of training and breeding champions. When we retired from the horse industry in 2008 and built what we thought would be our final home and barn, these two gray horses moved with us in the company of eight others. Were you to ask me then which horses I would end up calling mine, I wouldn't have named either one of the grays.

Thankfully, God is smarter than I am, and I quickly began to appreciate the wisdom and grace with which He gifted me with these two. Not only are Bo and Swizzle beautiful horses, but they have shown a desire above and beyond what I ever dreamed of in the level of their commitment to a relationship with me.

## Asti

Elegant Asti is one of the best-trained horses I have ever turned out, willing to give any rider the benefit of the doubt, and possibly the most valuable horse on the place if one were to perform an objective appraisal. I have logged hundreds of hours on her back as we worked through issue after issue together, mastering skill after skill. Asti is safe for the first ride of a grandchild but is also the perfect school mount to help my husband work on his equitation skills. I love Asti, but a part of her remains aloof, her greatest affections held in reserve for the visit of some little kid she's never met before. I guess I'm just too tall to deserve her full devotion.

## Baber and Copper

Copper is Baber's horse. I suppose this is the time to explain that I call my husband by our last name. When asked how he would like me to refer to him in this book, by "Baber" or "Larry," he was quick to select the former. I wasn't surprised. Baber does not like it when I call him by his given name. He never cared for his first name and for some reason he equates my use of it to a mother using her child's first and middle names when she is not particularly happy with them. So, Baber it is.

Copper has a couple of soundness issues that prevent me from being able to accomplish all I want to if he were one of "my" horses. He is a funny guy, sweet, and not terribly complicated. Copper and Baber get along famously for the most part, and I am pleased they found each other. Again, Copper is not the horse I thought my husband would be spending his life with, but God got it right again.

**Bo**

Bo is a five-year-old gray quarter horse gelding bred to work cattle. He wasn't even halter broke when I bought him in the middle of his two-year-old year. Unlike most gray horses who are born some other color, Bo was rose gray from the beginning. His coat is slick and full of dark dapples. His breeder told me that Bo was born with a lop ear and narcolepsy. They spent a great deal of time and money keeping the little guy going until he grew out of his issues. I am so grateful they did!

Something about the way Bo naturally engaged his body was intriguing to me when I first saw his photo, and the fact that he was cute and gray didn't hurt either. When we bought Copper as a long two-year-old, also untrained, I told him he would be auditioning to be "my horse." I told Bo the same thing.

With the sale of our ranch in the works, building a new house, barns, and fences on one of our remote hayfields, and Baber's elderly parents requiring most of our time, Bo had less than thirty rides during the first seven months I owned him. Needless to say, he did not progress rapidly. He was stiff in the face, reluctant to lope, and it was difficult to get him to go either fast or slow. He had a rapid, stiff trot and was pretty dedicated to not changing it. Surprisingly, one of the comments I hear most frequently now is how smooth Bo appears to be at the trot and lope— and he is. Bo and I worked on the most basic of basics when I had time to ride him. We weren't able to pay much attention to any of our horses for nearly twelve months before my in-laws passed away in spring of 2008.

However, once Bo and I had the opportunity to spend time together more consistently, our relationship blossomed. Bo learned obedience and respect. I learned to appreciate what a steady and secure personality he is. There were, however, times I thought he would never learn his leads. I had to teach him maneuvers that were way ahead of my plans in order to get him to lope in the lead requested. Once we started to click, it was amazing how quickly Bo added skills and retained all I taught him.

God gave me the right horse in Bo. I haven't begun to plumb the depths of what is possible for us. Every new thing I ask of him he does willingly and (eventually) well. If a particular maneuver proves more difficult to master, Bo keeps trying until we get the job done. We trust each other. We seek each other out. People remark on the relationship we share when they see us out on a ride or at a shooting competition. Bo and I have plans. In the meantime, he amazes me.

**Swizzle**

The last of the four horses grazing in the pasture outside my window is Swizzle, a three-year-old gray quarter horse filly bred to be a reining horse. Swizzle is not a tall horse. So far she is barely tall enough to be considered a horse and not a pony; but she is broad, sturdy, and a looker. All four of the horses grazing in the pasture are well fed and well muscled. There isn't a lightweight in the bunch, but Swizzle is probably more pony per inch than any of the rest, which says a lot considering the mass of the others. Swizzle is also cute. She has big, soft brown eyes; and though the gray hairs on her face will eventually prevent her white star and stripe from showing, the image they make is the reason I named her Swizzle. The star between her eyes twists about like a tiny tornado—a swizzle—before evening out as it continues down her face.

Swizzle is the only one of the four horses to come from our own breeding program. Asti, Copper, and Bo were all purchased with an eye toward possible resale. I trained them all and, surprisingly, they are still with us. We had intended to sell Swizzle as we did all our other foals, but the collapsing horse market and the issues she had when I tried to start her under saddle changed the course of her life. It changed the course of mine as well. All of our horses are bred to be champions. It is interesting to me that I can no longer readily remember the specifics of their individual pedigrees. Each of our horses is a member of our family, so the names on their registration papers don't seem to matter much anymore.

It was not that long ago that I hoped for a buyer for Swizzle. She was small, did not move the way I had hoped for, kept dinging herself up in the pasture, and when I first tried to ride her, I knew I was in trouble. Besides, we had too many horses, and I had others I loved more than Swizzle. Well, God has a way of arranging circumstances. Now I am blessed with Swizzle and have learned more than one lesson by the manner in which she became one of my amazing grays.

Swizzle was born a dark brown bay with a thick black mane and tail that rivals the hair on any My Pretty Pony toy horse. I always knew she was gray, but you couldn't tell from a distance until late in her two-year-old year. It is now obvious Swizzle is gray, her slick coat accessorized with heavy dark dapples. Swizzle's mane and tail are turning gray as well, which at this stage means mostly black with flaxen and gray hairs moving throughout her mane and her tail a lighter color at the bottom, still black at the top. Every year Swizzle will sport a different look until she finally turns white in later life. I am in no hurry. I plan on enjoying the journey Swizzle, Bo, and I will make together over the coming years.

Swizzle is amazing to me in much the same way Bo is, so together they are my amazing grays. Swizzle was always a sweet filly, easy to train and eager to learn. Much of her early life was spent in pasture with other foals and then as the youngest member of the herd once we moved to our retirement home. Indeed, as a yearling, Swizzle and Asti spent months together in pasture with two other mares. Asti adopted Swizzle, even allowing her to try and nurse, which I found quite odd. Asti has never had a foal, and Swizzle was in the middle of her yearling year. Was it stress that made them create such a close relationship? Any thought I have is only conjecture, so I'll never know the truth of their relationship.

Swizzle wasn't sold before it was time to start her under saddle so I brought her into the barn and began introducing her to new things. Swizzle had little foundation at the time, except the very minimums of yielding to pressure on her hip, leading with a rope around her neck, and finally learning to lead with a halter. She had always been good about getting her feet trimmed, never forgetting a thing between farrier visits. I expected Swizzle would be an easy, quick student and thought we would be riding together in no time though she had only been handled once every six weeks since she was weaned to trim her feet. The eighteen months between weaning and two-year-old training for Swizzle was just a blur of other obligations for us, so she and I had added very little to our relationship. But the few times I worked with her she was still sweet, eager to be with me, and learned her lessons easily and quickly.

Have I mentioned how quickly horses can humble humans? I spent lots of time messing around with Swizzle, but because I thought she was going to be so easy to start under saddle, I took more than a few shortcuts preparing her to be ridden. My program for starting colts is tried and true, but this time I didn't follow the program. Having moved to a new place without a training facility, I had only a barn and pasture to work with. Let's just say it never occurred to me that Swizzle could possibly be cold backed, lock up, and exhibit true talent as a bucking horse. All went well until the second time I got in the saddle. Being a quick study, by the *third* time I left the saddle without planning to, I knew I needed another plan. My fault. The only high point of this day was that the third time I was ejected from the saddle I landed on my feet!

So how did this wicked little bucking filly become one of my amazing grays? Grace. Swizzle is a gift of grace to me and having the time to build a right relationship with Swizzle is a gift of grace to her. Swizzle is indeed the filly I expected her to be. She prefers my company to her food, and that is saying a lot for a horse. Swizzle seeks my company even more than Bo does. She looks for me and is the first to run across the pasture if there is a chance for attention. Swizzle just wants to be near me and I have to smile every time I catch sight of her. She loves to work. She is sweet, and she continues to challenge me in ways that I am not challenged in other areas of my walk with the Lord. We are learning together. In fact, it is possible that Swizzle and I may exceed the achievements Bo and I will make. Time will tell. Our purpose is the journey we share. Each day of progressive relationship with my grays is a success in and of itself.

I cannot imagine two more perfect, and more different, partners than I have in my grays, Bo and Swizzle. There is one more reason I believe they are amazing: the Lord has used my relationship with them to help me understand my relationship with Him. Amazing grays, amazing grace. How can I separate the two?

# BUILDING FOUNDATION

*Therefore everyone who hears these words of mine and puts them into practice is like a wise man who built his house on the rock. The rains came down ... But it did not fall because it had its foundation on the rock.*

Matthew 7:24–25

*The dictionary is the only place success comes before work.*

Vince Lombardi

There is really no limit to what Bo and Swizzle will do for me if I am faithful and lead correctly. When you take the time to build a proper foundation, the only way left is up.

What all do I want from my amazing grays? Bo and Swizzle both have the proper foundation for all basic riding and good ground manners. How high a level do I want to prepare them for? Western riding? Reining? Dressage? What might I want to do on the ground? Tricks? High-level aires similar to the Lippizan stallions?

Perhaps bowing—it would make great photos and add to the foundation of responses we could build on in the future. If I taught Bo to bow, I could also get on him without using a mounting block. As you will discover later, I am an orthopedic disaster and could not pass the most basic pre-purchase evaluation. I do want to clarify that I have never been seriously injured by a horse. I can't, however, say that about motorcycles…so, I am a great advocate of mounting blocks, even for folks who are completely sound. They make life easier on both the rider and the horse. So, perhaps teaching Bo how to bow really is a great idea.

The trick to building foundation is the advance planning it requires. There is no substitute for a proper foundation. You can build a super nice garage on a six-inch-thick slab of concrete. However, if you buy the garage and then decide to build a four-story office building on that same six-inch concrete slab, you will encounter more than a few problems. You will have an inadequate foundation to support your plans. The same is true when building organizations, in education, and in horse training. It isn't a lengthy process to teach most horses to go forward, to stop, and to turn left and right. Most horses never progress much past these basics.

Should you ever want to show your horse in any type of competition, these basics will not be nearly enough foundation to get you from step one to step two. Training a horse is similar to learning ballroom dancing. Loosely speaking, there is the proper way, the classical way, and a modern or freestyle way. What is considered proper today evolved from the classical way, and freestyle always challenges existing boundaries and limits of creativity. Great dancers are able to successfully perform in any of the three ways.

Horsemanship and equine competition is very similar. There is the proper way, the classical way, and a freestyle way. Great horsemen can do all three. Unless you have dedicated a considerable amount of time and study to dancing, you won't have a clue about how to evaluate differences among the couples on the dance floor. Can you judge the execution of the steps, the line of the arms, the tilt of the head, the partnership between the dancers, the correctness, or lack thereof, in the actual performance?

Judging a "simple" class like Western Pleasure or Halter (conformation) correctly is really quite complex. In a Western Pleasure class, each horse and rider perform three gaits going one way in the arena, then reverse and do the same three gaits the other way. The three gaits are walk, jog, and lope. How difficult could that be to score?

Western Pleasure is actually very technical regardless of how simple it seems. Many riders compete in Western Pleasure and never truly understand what the judge looks for as he or she selects the winners and places the exhibitors from first to last. Are the horse's gaits true? Is the horse exhibiting "lift" in its shoulders? Is the performance consistent, each stride the same as the one before and the one after? Does the horse move in an easy, collected manner? Does the horse appear to present a pleasant picture, consistent frame, and natural head carriage, not too high or too low? Is the horse slow-legged and natural, or do the gaits appear to be manufactured?

Enough. Hopefully I have made the point that a huge amount of foundation goes into successful horse-rider relationships. This is equally true of our relationship with God. Without devoting a significant amount of time and study to this most important relationship, we will have no idea of the criteria he uses to judge us. Is dancing really simple? No. Is Western Pleasure really simple? No. Is life really simple? Just reading the rulebook in no way prepares one to dance or compete in equine competitions. Do you think just reading the Bible prepares you to be successful as a child of God? Once we accept that life is a bit more complicated than we first thought, we need to evaluate how strong our foundations are. What foundational planning have you done so far?

## Remodeling Is Always Messy

You may remember our elegant black mare, Asti. We bought her as a coming three-year-old. Our first thought was she might make a good show horse for my husband. Asti was sired by a reserve world champion western pleasure stallion and out of a producing mare. Asti is sixteen hands tall, true black with white chrome, and a real looker. I found Asti on the Internet and, not wishing to travel to Missouri where she was, I relied on a videotape to evaluate her potential. The video indicated she might have the gaits necessary to succeed as a pleasure horse. The gal representing her thought she had the temperament I was looking for. After having a Missouri vet do a pre-purchase examination, Asti came to Texas to begin her new life with us.

I loved her as soon as I saw her back out of the transport trailer. It was late in the evening, and she was in an unfamiliar place. Asti got off the trailer, followed me quietly and confidently into the barn, entered her new stall, put her head in the feeder, and started eating. Asti never lifted her head to scan for danger and sure appeared to be user-friendly; exactly what we wanted.

I have spent more time training Asti than any other horse in at least the past ten years, maybe fifteen. When she arrived in Texas, I discovered her foundation was full of holes and needed a lot of remedial work. She couldn't even lope around the round pen on her own without falling onto her front end. She had to keep speeding up in order to not fall down! When I tried to lunge her, she would zip out at an unbalanced gallop, and she actually did fall down numerous times. The good news is Asti could hit the dirt sprawled like a spider and still come up sound every time. I had to undo all the training Asti came with, which wasn't a great deal and mostly wrong. The biggest problem was her lack of confidence and the failure of leadership from a previous trainer. On the ground she had really good manners, except for being cinchy (getting seriously annoyed when the saddle girth was tightened).

Eventually Asti and I began to build a new foundation of relationship. Time, repetition, and consistency expanded her repertoire of skills. Asti wasn't always that happy about learning, but she wasn't all that resistant either. She did have days, though, where she was just a pill. Over the next couple of years she became very trustworthy and really broke, but my schedule didn't allow the opportunity to really finish her for the show pen.

In the meantime, my husband seemed to have found his own horse, so Asti didn't appear to be needed there anymore. We were in the process of downsizing and entered a contract to sell her. An odd set of circumstances kept her in our barn, none being her fault. Now we are thrilled it worked out that way. The horse my husband hoped would be his companion for life ended up with too many soundness issues to keep. A good home was found for that horse, but my husband was heartbroken and discouraged.

Asti is a lot of fun to ride and tries to figure out what each rider wants. She also loves children. I'm about fifty years too old to really appeal to her. My grandchildren can ride her. Any novice can ride her. With a little tuning, she is just a good ride for anyone, even into many upper-level maneuvers. As it turns out, Asti is exactly the horse my husband needed to help him work on his horsemanship skills.

Asti is the equivalent of a law-abiding and pleasant person. While she is admirable and lovely, she does not seek a committed relationship with her master. How many of us fail to achieve our full potential because we ignored or just gave lip service to God one too many times? He is faithful to keep and cherish us—as I do Asti—but the commitment on her end never quite equaled my "offer." Asti is wonderful, but she just does not see me in the same way Bo and Swizzle do.

*Asti*

One day not long ago Bo came up to me as the horses were coming in to the barn for breakfast. Usually he waits till the mares are in their stalls and then places himself at my right elbow and "heels" until we get to his gate. This day, for whatever reason, Bo lipped my hand. Well, that was disrespectful way past anything that could be tolerated, so I smacked him hard on his hip with my walking stick. Did he run away? Of course not. He immediately adjusted his attitude and became obedient again. Did I hold that little incident against him? Not at all. Love doesn't change. Bo repented, I forgave him, and it was as if it never happened. My grays may be amazing, but they're not perfect and never will be. That's part of what makes our relationship so exciting.

## Minnie

I remember a cat we had at the ranch we named Minnie. She was a pretty little thing, a calico; caramel, brown and black on a pure white coat. She showed up as an older kitten, taking up residence in the dog kennel about one hundred feet from the house. Minnie kept my husband company as he worked on equipment or did chores around the house and nearby areas. She was sweet, attentive, and pretty darn cute. Of course, we adopted her. My husband is a cat guy. I like cats, but I'm more of a dog person. If any of you are cat people, you will understand the attraction my husband felt to this kitten.

It is our practice to geld, spay, or neuter any animal except the horses in our breeding program. When we made the decision to adopt her into the family, Minnie went to the vet to be spayed. She returned the next afternoon and was installed back into the dog kennel to be safe and secure. I wanted to be sure she recovered well and was comfortable, so I kept an eye on her from my window.

Now that I was paying closer attention, it soon became apparent that Minnie was afraid to come out of the kennel if there was no one out there keeping her company. She had to cross over in front of the shop building to reach the water bowl, a trip of about thirty feet. One day as I watched, Minnie began to slowly make her way to the water dish, hugging the ground and looking about her in fear as she agonized over every step. The slightest rustle of leaves would send her running back to the kennel. Poor little Minnie. We took pity on her and made a decision we thought we would never make. We moved Minnie into the house. Years before, in Arizona, we had a house cat and had worked out the litter box problem. "Never again," we promised each other. No house cats. And yet, here was little Minnie in the house and so was her litter box.

I suppose I shouldn't have been surprised. We have two big dogs that we adopted for the sole purpose of living outside and chasing off varmints. Eventually, both dogs ended up as couch potatoes, sleeping in our room. Reiner, it seems, is afraid of the dark; and Blue has skin issues with heat. Neither of these big guys showed any aptitude to identify a varmint, much less scare one off.

So Minnie, the pretty, attentive little kitten moved in. As time passed, she became more demanding at meal times. She waited by her dish each morning, and I almost thought I saw her tapping her paw as she impatiently waited to be fed. We taught Minnie to use the pet door so she could come and go as she pleased. Thankfully, this allowed us to retire the litter box. Minnie shared our bed at night with our other four little bedmates: three miniature dachshunds and one scruffy little terrier from the Omaha pound.

How did it all work out? Was Minnie, the little rescued kitten, happy in her circumstances? I'm sure she was. She also became more and more entitled to the services provided by her handmaiden and butler (that would be me and my husband). Minnie felt entitled to food on demand, cat cookies (she could still be cute when she wanted to), and free rein, or should I say, reign, of the house. Minnie also became amazingly aloof, keeping in mind, of course, that she was, after all, a cat. The butler and handmaiden were no longer allowed to touch her majesty, Queen Minnie. She wouldn't give us the time of day unless there was food in our hand. If we managed to trap her in a corner, we could pick her up and she didn't fight us, but she was never in the mood to sit with us anymore.

## Relationships Are Not Unilateral

Our relationship with Minnie was strictly one way. Minnie expected us to give, give, give. She expected to offer nothing in return but a hearty appetite. Anything more was just too much. Minnie threw up on the furniture. She scratched the daylights out of the few upholstered pieces of furniture we owned. We couldn't even lock her back outdoors without also locking out the six dogs. Minnie had really worn out her welcome, yet we didn't want to give up on her.

Minnie used to be connected to us, or so we thought. She looked to us for safety. She relied on us to meet her needs. We did. Now she was so secure we became servants rather than the saviors we had been to the scared, little stray kitten. Minnie grew up and adopted the belief that she was somehow entitled to all she desired. To try and repair the situation, I made a point of trapping her once a day and spending time with her. Please remember, I am not a cat person. Minnie figured it out and stopped waiting at her food dish. I had to get more creative. Each day I caught her and sat on the sofa with her on my lap. I sat and stroked her gently as I tried to get her to enjoy being with us again. Minnie would relax and sit quietly. But as soon as I took away my hand, the opportunity to exit presented itself and she was gone. Over and over we repeated this exercise. Nothing ever changed.

Decision time came. We sold the ranch and were preparing to move into a brand new house. There was no way we were going to take Queen Minnie to our new house and be subject to her demands for the next dozen years or so.

Minnie forgot who saved her. Minnie forgot the giver.

Her sense of entitlement grew to a level that judged the gifts we gave as nothing more than what was due her. We tried to save the relationship and put it back into order. She wouldn't cooperate. Minnie went to the pound.

How must God feel when He looks at us? Do we remember who saved us? Have we come to believe we are entitled to all we receive? Have we forgotten the source of all our blessings? There is still time to work out our relationship with Him. If we don't, well, you know where Minnie went.

Thankfully, my grays are not like either Asti or Minnie. Asti is with us for the rest of her life. She may not offer 110 percent to our relationship, but she sure meets us more than halfway. We enjoy her, she is beautiful, and she has a job.

Bo and Swizzle are daily blessings. They learn from me, and I learn from them. We will continue to build upon our firm foundation. The sky is the limit. Perhaps we'll begin working on the bowing thing soon. It's a great adventure.

# FAITH IN THE UNSEEN

*Jesus said, "Come." And when Peter had come down out of the boat, he walked on water to go to Jesus.*

Matthew 14:29

*I know when the proposition comes from God because of its quiet insistence. When I have to weigh the pros and cons, and doubt and debate come in, I am bringing in an element that is not of God, and I come to the conclusion that the suggestion was not a right one.*

Oswald Chambers

Loyalty to Jesus means that I have to step out where I do not see anything.

Evidence of this loyalty from a horse, this faith in the unseen, is exhibited when we ask horses to step backwards out of a trailer when they can't see the ground, or to step into a water box when they have no way of knowing if there is a bottom. Our horse knows that we mean for it to obey our request when we keep a quiet, gentle pressure on until it obeys. If our training skills are not advanced enough, or our lesson plan not well enough defined, we may be tentative or inconsistent in our requests causing the horse to become unsure.

Horses in this situation usually select from one of three options. The first choice is for the horse to do nothing until more clear direction is received from the trainer. The second in the list of choices is for the horse to weigh its options, make a best guess at what the trainer is indeed asking it to do, and then make a good faith attempt to comply. The last option is for the horse to decide that the leadership being offered is insufficient and to make a completely independent decision, judging the trainer to be incompetent and not worthy of consideration.

Human trainers are certainly capable of indecision or error. God, however, is never indecisive or in error. In the horse-human relationship, we must always give the horse the benefit of our doubt. A horse is truly seldom wrong. Horses are consistent to a fault, often to the great frustration of humans who don't understand them. The blame for bad behavior or wrong response on the part of the horse can nearly always be laid at the feet of the trainer. Occasionally a horse will just say no—but it is usually obvious and can even be funny. We have to correct them, but gently and firmly.

A perfect example of one such instance involves Arizona Sky, my very first horse. At the time I was a business consultant, speaker, and very active in my community. I also had very bad knees and was unable to do much vigorous exercise. My doctors didn't want me to do anything that required me to stand or put pressure on my knees. Truthfully, I wasn't capable of much even if I wanted to just tough it out. As a fairly young person with a lifelong habit of exercise and athletic pursuits I was looking for an outlet for my excess physical energy. I tried flying small aircraft, but an inner ear issue grounded me almost immediately.

One Saturday I told my husband I was looking for a stable. He asked me why. I told him I needed a place for my horse. Being an intelligent guy he asked, "What horse?" I told him I was getting a horse and would need a stall the next day. Suffice it to say, I became the proud owner of a young, mostly untrained, liver chestnut filly on Sunday. By evening she was safely housed in her new home, a boarding stable a few miles from our house.

Over the next six months I learned more horse training concepts, mastered the most basic of basics, and spent some time every day with my filly. Nebraska in winter gets a bit on the cold side. Many days Arizona Sky and I simply messed around in the indoor round pen trying to stay warm as temperatures dipped to 35 degrees below zero. I rode Arizona Sky a lot that winter in my snowmobile suit, the ice on the metal doors of the enclosed arena more than six inches thick. We never missed a day's lesson when I was in town. I taught Arizona Sky how to learn. She taught me to respect "horse."

*My first teacher, Arizona Sky*

Once she had mastered "learning to learn" and I learned consistency and precision, we moved on to little tricks of all kinds. In our routine, I would give Arizona Sky a cue and show her the response I had in mind. When she didn't give the correct response, I would send her out at a trot around the round pen to let her know she had missed something. It was a long cold winter, and Arizona Sky and I spent hours and hours in that indoor round pen together learning tricks and building a relationship. We occasionally collected little audiences on weekends and did our little shows.

Well, as I mentioned earlier, sometimes a horse just says no. One day Arizona Sky and I were teaching each other in the indoor round pen. We were practicing dancing. Dancing in this case meant the same as heeling does with a dog. There was no halter and lead rope involved. No matter what I did or how quickly I whirled around and changed directions—right, left, forward, or backward—Arizona Sky was to stay exactly in heel position. One of the most memorable moments of my horse training career occurred the day Arizona Sky just said, "No."

Our dance routine was getting to be pretty fast and furious. I expected Arizona Sky to stop, back, roll right, swing left, faster and faster. She was keeping up pretty well until she stopped, deliberately nipped my right elbow with her lips, looked directly into my eyes as if to say "I quit," and immediately took herself to the perimeter of the round pen and started trotting around to correct herself! It was hilarious. I also changed the lesson plan for the rest of the day.

The relationship between God and man is similar. You must give God the benefit of your doubt. I guarantee He has no doubt. If you feel that "quiet insistence" you must yield and obey. If you are unsure, you have the same three options a horse has in the same circumstances. Again, they are, first, to do nothing until you receive more clear instruction. The difficult thing here is to determine why the instruction isn't clear. Second, you can try to figure out what the Lord wants of you, what His will is. His requests are seldom loud enough to be heard above the raucous noise of busy lives. If you are unsure, get quiet and give yourself a chance to hear clearly. Unlike a horse, you can actively seek out the Lord through prayer. If the answer doesn't come immediately, you are no worse off and you can just go back to waiting patiently for a further cue.

Sadly, this final option is the one most often selected by humans. If we don't find God's presence or message coming in loud and clear, or we assume a position of tell me now, or else, the failure to receive the specific and obvious response we demand causes us to decide that either God doesn't exist, that He has somehow failed us, or that God just isn't all that powerful after all, and we dismiss Him entirely.

Always give your horse the benefit of your doubt when his response is not what you expected. Redouble your efforts to be clear and precise in the requests you make. Precise results require precise requests. It is a sure bet that the horse's failure to respond as hoped for is the fault of the trainer. The result we pursue is right relationship. The loyalty we desire from our horses is built upon a strong foundation of respect, consistency, security, and trust. Strive to deserve your horse's loyalty and trust. These are your best tools for getting your horse to step out when it is unsure. Arizona Sky learned to learn and she learned to trust me.

Always give the Lord the benefit of your doubt as well. Increase the time and emphasis you dedicate to listening and reading his Word. I guarantee the fault in communication is always yours. You will find no richer relationship than that with Jesus Christ and no better role model for a leader than our Savior. Learn to be worthy of the faith your horse puts in your leadership.

*There are unknown worlds of knowledge in brutes; and whenever you mark a horse or a dog with a peculiarly mild, calm, deep-seated eye, you may be sure he is an Aristotle or Kant, tranquilly speculating upon the mysteries in man. No philosopher so thoroughly comprehends us as dogs and horses. They see through us at a glance... But there is a touch of divinity even in brutes, and a special halo about a horse that should forever exempt him from indignities. As for those majestic, magisterial truck-horses of the docks, I would as soon think of striking a judge on the bench as to lay violent hand upon their holy hides.*

Herman Melville, "Redburn. His First Voyage," 1849

# DISPUTABLE THINGS

*If it is possible, as much as depends on you, live peaceably with all men.*

Romans 12:18

*The optimist says the cup is half full. The pessimist says the cup is half empty. The child of God says, "My cup runneth over."*

Anonymous

For ten years I operated a commercial horse training facility on the north side of Phoenix. Not only did I train there, but over the years a number of other trainers also based their businesses at our ranch.

For a time, two independent dressage trainers headquartered with me. I boarded their horses as well as their clients' and students' horses. I established the ground rules up front in hopes of preventing any friction between the competing trainers.

Here are the ground rules that were in effect at my training facility:

1. No blood.

2. Everyone on the place was expected to get along like a family. If problems arose, we would solve them peacefully, equitably, and respectfully.

3. All horses must be kept up to my standards of basic healthcare and handled with educated and humane treatment.

4. Loose dogs only allowed with prior permission.

5. If disputes ever became serious, it was understood that I would never have to leave because I actually lived there. Assurances were given that should the situation call for separation, I would actively help the other trainer find a better situation elsewhere.

All went well for a time, and then the murmuring began. "Lynn, Lynn!" a dressage student would breathlessly begin, "the other trainer is abusing a horse! What are you going to do?" The first time or two this happened I asked the appropriate questions to determine what the actual situation was and what it specifically was the reporting student believed (or their trainer led them to believe) to be abusive treatment. After carefully investigating the allegation of abuse, it was always the case that the two trainers simply used different training methods to teach horses similar skills. This is perfectly normal. I have always said that the best horse trainer is the one who knows the most ways to teach the same thing. Horses are as unique as people. A technique that works well with one horse will cause nothing but resistance in another. What one horse thinks is punishment another horse will think is fun. Reminds you of your kids, doesn't it?

It soon became apparent that the differences in methods used by the two trainers were becoming a cause of division among their students. I called a barn-wide meeting for the dressage trainers, their clients, and students. This was the first of what became dozens, if not hundreds, of instances where I used my horse religion speech.

## The Horse Religion Speech

Let's assume you have a fascination with religion so you visit different places of worship. One week you attend a Catholic mass, the next week a Jewish synagogue. The following week finds you researching at a Buddhist temple, the next week a Baptist tent revival. Your investigations take you in turn to observances of Muslims, Mormons, Wiccas, Shintos, and Methodists. By this time, you are so confused about the topic of religion that your head is ready to explode.

Each religion is absolutely certain they are correct. Yet they cannot all be right—it isn't possible given the drastic differences in their belief systems. Yet each member who is convicted by the teachings of his faith is truly betting his life on it.

The same, I believe, is true if one is fascinated with horses. You pursue your interest in horses by reading books, articles, and blogs. You watch countless hours of videos, DVDs, and television shows. You spend a small fortune attending clinics, taking lessons, and drive hours to see yet another well-known clinician speak. You will eventually arrive in a similar place as the person who was interested in religion. Each trainer and his or her followers are absolutely certain they are correct—they may even have great success to prove it. Yet they cannot all be right; it just isn't possible given the often-dramatic differences in their belief systems.

After I explained to the clients and students that neither dressage trainer was guilty of abuse, I concluded my remarks to both trainers and the others in this way: "My advice to you is to find people who believe the same things you do about horses. Stick with them, and give everybody else religious freedom."

As Paul wrote in Acts, "If it is possible, as much as depends on you, live peaceably with all men." The critical phrase is "as depends on you." There are absolute truths in Scripture that to a Christian are simply not open for discussion. The remainders are subject to interpretation. Unless the undisputable matters are involved, choose peace with others over dispute. Always give others the benefit of your doubt.

The same is true in the horse world. There are absolute truths which no amount of discussion will ever change. The rest is open to opinion and disagreement. On these matters learn to be tolerant of others. You don't have to agree, and you don't have to participate. Just like religion, stay with those who hold similar beliefs to yours, and leave the others in peace.

Many things in Christianity and horsedom are truly situational or are well met with a variety of options, each having its own merit. Should one worship on Sunday morning or Wednesday night? Do you really believe this question has only one absolutely correct answer? Of course not. You may even find your schedule requires you to make changes from your historically preferred weekly worship schedule from time to time.

Does a horse need to be clipped? Is a gaited horse better than a non-gaited horse? Should horses be shod? Should horses wear blankets in the winter? Should Sunday school be taught before or during the worship service? Should communion be served with grape juice or wine? Should Christians dance?

These are all questions about debatable issues. Find the people who share your belief systems about God and horses; give the others religious freedom.

# KEEP IT SIMPLE

*The entrance of Your words gives light; it gives understanding to the simple.*

Psalm 119:130

*It is opinions of our own which make us stupid; when we are simple we are never stupid, we discern all the time.*

Oswald Chambers

*Where in the world can man find nobility without pride, Friendship without envy, Or beauty without vanity? Here, where grace is served with muscle and strength by gentleness confined, he serves without servility; he has fought without enmity. There is nothing so powerful, nothing less violent. There is nothing so quick, nothing more patient.*

Ronald Duncan, "The Horse," 1954

My horses help me see with eyes of simplicity—this is one of the gifts I receive from Bo and Swizzle. They allow me to see through the eyes of a horse. Horses allow us to joyfully experience the uncommon unity of maturity, nobility and strength with child-like simplicity, honesty, and trust.

Horses are direct. They do not dissemble; they "say" what they mean. You will never get more honest feedback of your leadership ability than from a horse. The body of a pauper hits the dirt every bit as hard as the body of a prince when a horse bucks them off. Horses do not care what you look like. A horse's only interest in your net worth is your ability to keep fresh hay and grain coming. Your family tree is of less interest to the horse than the fly crawling up their stall door. How much political clout you wield gains you nothing with a horse. It's just you and the horse. They will judge you solely on your actions. How refreshing. Can you make this same statement about most of your friends and family?

## Getting the Upper Hoof

Horses teach more humans how to behave than humans teach horses. When an inexperienced or dull human tries to teach a horse and the horse does not learn, the human calls the horse stupid. The truth is the horse won. Clinton Anderson was the first person I heard who put the horse-human relationship into such simple terms: "He who controls the feet wins." In so many cases, the feet that move are the feet of the human.

It is the opinions of humans that blur truth and add complication to relationships where none need exist. The horse is simple. When talking about training between horse and man, horses can be more effective in getting their desired result from the human than the human from the horse. Humans talk, humans pontificate, while the horse merely looks at them with amusement or disdain. Horses lean on you, they ignore you, they step into your space, and your feet move! They won.

## The Stupidity of Pride

We humans lose our simplicity as we become more highly educated in worldly things. How God must laugh at us with our delusions of grandeur, unless His emotion is more one of disgust. One part of a valuable education is the ability to discern the relative worth of information or concepts presented by others. In our stupidity we have lost the compass that keeps us properly directed in our ability to evaluate material and opinion as we absorb it. When teachers present students with opinion disguised as fact, students are frequently unable to recognize the difference.

It is human nature to be vain and prideful; it is not the nature of the horse. My favorite illustration of the stupidity of pride is that of Naaman told in 2 Kings, chapter 5. Naaman, if you recall, was a great commander and valiant soldier. He was also a leper. In all his finery, with horses and chariots, Naaman went to the prophet Elisha to be healed. Elisha sent a messenger out to tell Naaman to wash seven times in the Jordan River and be healed. Naaman got mad because Elisha had not seen him personally and didn't perform the instant on-demand cure he had in mind. Not only that, but Naaman had a very low opinion of the Jordan River.

Luckily for Naaman, one of his servants was not so filled with pride and self-regard. The servant said, "If the prophet had told you to do some great thing, would you not have done it? Why then won't you just go wash and be cleaned?" Of course, Naaman did and was healed. What is it with humans? We are more concerned with station and status at times than life itself. The horse is too simple to be so foolish.

Today, people are so limited in their outlook and so arrogantly dedicated to their own opinions that they call you stupid (or worse) should you disagree with them. In today's social and political debate, it has become commonplace to throw verbal bombs as weapons meant to silence the opposition. The speaker today pretends to stand on legal or moral high ground while all the time pitching mud and filth in the face of any who disagree. The civility of agreeing to disagree is fast becoming a memory. How odd these warriors appear as they attempt to elevate humanity by fighting dirty. A horse would never do such an ignoble thing.

Some horse owners think that when a horse doesn't do as they ask, the horse is stupid. Years ago Baber was going to rinse off Sugar, our first broodmare. Now Sugar had been hauled across the country and to innumerable shows before we even bought her. Sugar knew more about wash racks than Baber did. When he and Sugar were about five feet from the broad, open, concrete slab, she stopped. Baber tried to pull her, coax her, and tap her behind the elbow. She didn't move. Dumb horse? Nope. Inexperienced leader. I don't know what Sugar's motivation was; she certainly wasn't upset. I suppose she decided to see if she could be boss. It worked. Baber asked, "What's wrong with her?" I said, "She's being a pig." I walked over and told Sugar what I thought of her behavior. She sweetly walked into the wash rack while Baber fumed behind us.

Every day, or maybe even every minute, a horse is accused of being stupid when it will not load up into a horse trailer. Sometimes the horse is frightened; sometimes the horse is just a better trainer than the human. The horse has taught its owner to offer oats, carrots, cookies, or whatever, before it condescends to get into the trailer. Many fat and happy dogs and horses are so "dumb" they just won't eat plain old dog or horse food. Oats are cooked, bran is mashed, and "ponykins" is served dinner. I expect there are many parents who might read this and wonder if their children are "playing" them. They may be right.

In the battle for simplicity and frankness, horses win. Let me tell you about the freedom and blessing simplicity can add to a relationship. A number of years ago my husband discovered that he could be direct and honest without the sky falling on him. Someone at church had asked him to dress up in costume for a play and he said no. When asked why, he quite honestly replied, "Because I don't want to." Although it was a bit unexpected for the dear lady who received his refusal, I have been greatly blessed by this new, straightforward approach.

Many times during the past twenty-five years I have run into resistance from my husband to some particular event or project and verbally searched and inquired of him, trying to understand where his apparent objection came from or why we were so obviously unable to communicate. The day of liberation came when he gave me the same response he had given the lady at church: he just didn't want to. How freeing such honest simplicity is. I now had the complete story; I didn't have to keep coming up with question after question in my (wasted) attempts to figure out why I wasn't getting anywhere. We get so caught up sometimes in trying not to be negative that we create hard feelings and frustration by wandering aimlessly around a subject when "no" would have resolved the matter quickly and cleanly.

A response of "no" is a clear indication that a person is unwilling. No amount of explanation will create willingness. Once you reach sufficient understanding to know you are both on the same page, willingness must be addressed with a radically different strategy than inability. In most cases, folks, just drop it. You may notice as you progress through *Amazing Grays, Amazing Grace* that I do not directly address spousal or equal relationships. Our relationship with God is not one of equals, nor is mine with Bo and Swizzle. My message here is one of simplicity. *Amazing Grays, Amazing Grace* isn't offered as insight or instruction on life with your spouse, although I hope you may find a helpful nugget of truth along the way.

**Nothing Compares with God**

The comparison I make between the good trainer-horse relationship and the God-man relationship is meaningful, yet inherently flawed. Such analogy can only go so far. No other relationship is worthy of direct comparison to one with God. However, God allows me to use the trainer-horse relationship to more easily keep my thoughts simple and focused, and as much as is humanly possible, see with His eyes. My relationships with Bo and Swizzle give me a perspective I would not otherwise have. I am able to stand at the bottom of the staircase and look up at the same time I stand at the top of the staircase and look down. I know how the shoes fit of both leader and follower. We learn from other humans daily, but man is just not as good a study partner as a horse. The opinions, prejudices, and influences all men bring to relationships confuse issues. You may trust that the horse will give you an honest and consistent response from which you may judge your own behavior.

When confronted with complex interpersonal or group dynamics there are occasions when I am at a loss to know how to proceed to successfully resolve issues with an individual or to attain team goals. I find that by assigning the same situation to a herd of horses all my mental cobwebs are swept away and I am able to formulate workable plans. Horses are simple. The simplicity of a child is a requirement of entry through the narrow gate. In Matthew 18:3 Jesus simply says, "I tell you the truth, unless you change and become like little children, you will never enter the kingdom of heaven."

Embrace simplicity and rediscover your child-like joy.

# FOLLOW THE LEADER

*We are more than conquerors through Him that loved us.*

Romans 8:37

*Courage is not the absence of fear, but rather the judgment that something else is more important than fear.*

Ambrose Redmoon (James Neal Hollingsworth 1933–1996)

Did you know that a horse has two distinctly different sides to its personality? Unlike human brains, the two separate halves of a horse's brain are not physically connected to each other. When a horse learns something with its right eye, the left eye has no clue what the right eye learned, and vice versa.

The two sides of a horse's brain are the thinking side and the reacting side. All good horse trainers are well aware of this peculiarity of horse anatomy and consider it when developing their training programs. The right side of the horse's brain is the natural side, the side that reacts from instinct. The left side of the horse's brain is the thinking side, the side that is trainable and open to relationships. This makes sense even from a non-scientific perspective in that we normally work with a horse on their near side, their left side. Many horses are not handled regularly from the off side, the right side, leaving that side of the brain in a more natural state. The most successful relationship with a horse is one that is modeled in a way that makes sense to the natural or reacting side of the brain.

Our goal as good horse trainers is for the reacting side of the horse's brain to accept us as herd leader. We build on this instinctual foundation of relationship by training the thinking side of the brain. As the relational side of the brain begins to be more dominant, the purely reactive behavior of the horse starts to diminish. Innate herd mentality hardwires the natural side of the brain to play follow-the-leader. If the leader is calm, the herd will be calm. If the leader is insecure, the herd members will also be insecure. Humans who resort to displays of anger and frustration when they work with their horses are telegraphing insecurity and danger to the horse. Inconsistency and lack of clear direction also equates with insecurity to the horse. Horses, like most animals and people, are naturally attracted to calm, confident personalities. One must be worthy to be a good herd leader. In horse-human relationships, the human is responsible for the safety of the horse, not the other way around.

**Fight or Flight**

When confronted with conflict or other perceived danger, the horse as a prey animal will enter the fight-or-flight mode. Having the natural brain of a prey animal, the horse will almost always choose flight. Usually the fight model will only click in if the horse is constrained from flight—backed into a corner or confined in a small area.

Another exception to flight as the response of choice would be fighting another horse to establish dominance.

Humans also have the fight-or-flight response system built into our basic makeup. We also have both a thinking side and a reacting side. As Paul tells us in Romans 8, the Christian mind is actually different from the non-Christian mind. The Christian mind I refer to here is one in right relationship with God. While extreme circumstances will cause most non-Christians to react to a seemingly desperate situation by releasing critical levels of adrenaline into their bloodstream—fear causing the fight-or-flight response to engage—the same extreme circumstance's effect on a Christian may not produce as much as a significant increase in blood pressure.

The Christian is not *unaware* of the situation; the Christian is *undaunted* by the situation.

Many times a particular set of circumstances will cause a "natural" horse or person to react in fear, to run or fight, seemingly for their lives. In contrast, however, the secure horse, the secure Christian, may not even acknowledge that same stressor as being anything of concern at all. It just wasn't a big enough deal to even register as a conscious event. At other times, Christians are aware, but they think about the circumstance. They do not merely react. The reactive side of a horse's personality triggers fear, just as it can with humans.

Confident horses and secure Christians seldom react in fear; they are trained by relationship to use the thinking side of their personality. We consider, we process, we lean upon our understanding and confidence in our leader. God is responsible for those really big things. The horse trainer, too, is responsible for the big decisions. We are calm because our leader is calm. We are secure because our leader is secure. In the barn, Bo and Swizzle gently chew their hay knowing they are safe. Christians drift off to sleep knowing that God is awake, keeping watch over them as they sleep.

Consider the sad circumstance of Stephen Curtis Chapman's family who lost their beloved five-year-old daughter and sister, Maria, on May 21, 2008. In a completely freak accident, Maria's older brother Will, ran over his sister as she ran to meet him on the driveway. Maria died as a result of her injuries. If you've not had the gift of experiencing Mr. Chapman's inspirational music, I recommend it to you. Mr. Chapman is a highly regarded and awarded Christian singer/songwriter who has greatly blessed me with his musical service to the Lord. As of 2007, Mr. Chapman had sold more than ten million albums, nine of them gold or platinum.

Did this tragedy break the Chapman family? No. Did they suffer from it? Yes. Did it trigger the fight-or-flight response? Will's first reaction to the events of that day was to run, to flee, but his family wouldn't let him go. Mr. Chapman was immediately concerned that the family not lose two children that day, the innocent son as well as the beloved youngest daughter. On *Good Morning America*, Mr. Chapman said they did not allow this tragedy to remove their faith in the Lord. This faith in the Lord is "the hope that we are anchored to in the midst of just what sometimes seems unbearable." Grief at their loss today, but joy, nonetheless, at their future reunion with Maria. Most families not securely connected to Christ would have simply reacted, exhibiting fight-or-flight behavior.

(GMA web article of 8/6/08 by Janice Johnston and Emily Yacus.)

"Fight" is the response displayed when one family member blames another family member for a tragedy. Sometimes blaming God for a loss is a manifestation of the fight response. Many families may ultimately fracture as a result of such a tragic blow. When reacting in a flight response, people might escape by sinking into a great depression, great denial, or by actually physically removing themselves from the family.

The proof of Paul's message, that we are more than conquerors through Christ, plays out daily in the Christian body by the power, comfort, and peace Christ offers us. This peace is one of the strongest evangelical tools Christians have to impact non-believers. "How," the unbeliever marvels, "can that person, that family, survive such tragedy? And not merely survive, but praise God in the midst of it?"

Once they ask this question, non-believers will generally follow with one of these two conclusions as they attempt to comprehend this nearly impossible-to-understand picture. They will either conclude the Christian response of sorrow-joy to be proof of a mental illness or delusion, or they will feel a quiet, internal tug that brings them to ask, "How can I get what they have?"

If you think such a response is delusional, all we can do is pray for you. If you are fortunate enough, blessed enough, to feel that tug, ask a Christian to share Christ with you. If possible, ask the very person who modeled this active faith of sorrow-joy to you. The Chapman's told their story publicly for this very purpose. Such an inquiry about the saving grace of Christ would not increase their sorrow; such inquiry would increase their joy. We can never give another person what we have found ourselves, but we can stir in them a desire to find it for themselves.

Does this make sense to you? Let me apply this concept to horses. Sometimes it is easier to grasp a concept if it is a bit further removed from our own experience, allowing for a more objective perspective.

## Becoming Fearless

A horse securely bonded to its trainer/leader will not exhibit the same fight-or-flight response to any one particular stimulus as will a horse without such relationship. The horse need not even be with its trainer to be exempt from concern about a situation that could cause panic in another horse. The minds of the two horses are actually different.

Horses often react violently to sudden noises or movements that trigger their flight response. If they didn't, horses would have been eaten into extinction by predators centuries ago. A sudden movement might be a mountain lion preparing to pounce on to their backs; the smart horse will run first and check out the facts later. That odd noise could be a rattlesnake waiting to strike. Once they've bolted to a safe distance, horses will turn and see if they were right. Better safe than sorry. Such is the nature of a prey animal.

Why don't my horses get too excited about such things? They've learned that sudden noises and formerly spooky stuff won't harm them. They believe I won't put them in a position to be eaten. They are right. Would they survive in the wild? I don't know. Horses that have truly learned to rely on humans tend to remain so, even if returned to the wild. Shame on humans when such a thing happens. A story was told in the *Quarter Horse News* a year or so ago by one columnist who had gone camping with her husband and their horses. When they woke in the morning, about fifteen "wild horses" were there, waiting to get in the trailer and "go home." How difficult it was for the horse-loving columnist and her husband to have to drive these lonely horses away in order to load their own into the trailer so they could quickly drive off as the abandoned horses tried to regroup and return.

My horses are fortunate. I will never abandon them. Christians are doubly blessed. There is none more faithful than our Lord.

As Bo and Swizzle learn to trust me, that old flight or fight response gradually weakens until it rarely, if ever, surfaces. I deal with the thinking side of their personalities. The process is one of creating trust, building foundation, proving my leadership, then maintenance, maintenance, maintenance. Each lesson builds upon the last. Tests become more difficult as I apply greater and greater pressure to check on my gray's responses. I crack a whip at their side; they just stand there. I shoot .45 caliber guns from their backs; they could care less. I throw things at my horses, noisy things, and they just look at me. If I am not concerned, neither are they. They are becoming fearless.

A few weeks ago I was preparing to rinse Bo off after a sweaty ride. He stood quietly in the indoor concrete-walled wash rack waiting for me to get organized. I expect my horses to stay where I put them, so Bo wasn't even tied in the wash rack. The spray nozzle wasn't on the hose, so I fumbled with the quick-connect ends to attach the pressure nozzle to the hose. I lay the hose and nozzle down on the concrete floor and turned on the water. Not having correctly attached the nozzle and hose, the sudden pressure of the water shot the nozzle off the end of the hose like a projectile with a noise that sounded like a bomb.

This all occurred right at Bo's hind feet. I fully expected him to bolt out of there and head off to a safe distance before checking to see if I had survived the blast. I am both humbled and ashamed to say that I was surprised when his only reaction was to clamp his tail tightly to his butt and assume a readiness posture as he waited for me to give direction. He never moved a foot. I was humbled by this testament to the change in Bo's nature. I am ashamed that I was surprised. So, what did I do next? I pretended that nothing unusual had happened, paid more attention to how I connected the nozzle, and gave Bo his bath.

In mounted shooting, we have to carry balloons. If you don't think that is a testament to the trust our horses place in our relationship, try it yourself on a new horse. Actually, don't try it unless you know what you're doing. Balloons move, especially on windy days, and they will actually "touch" a horse when he isn't expecting it. I've seen the flight response kick in more than once when a horse met a balloon. Do you really appreciate the confidence a horse must have in its rider to carry a parade flag? Horses with great leaders even learn to ignore helicopters hovering over their heads, firecrackers going off at their heels, and most any other scenario you can come up with.

As children of God, we are changed creatures by the relationship we share with Him. The new habits born of this relationship allow us to truly understand what Jesus means when he tells us to "Fear not."

## Corrie Ten Boom

Many of you may already be familiar with Corrie ten Boom, a Dutch Christian survivor of the Nazi concentration camps. Her book, *The Hiding Place*, tells her family's story of hiding Jews in their home during World War II. Their efforts saved an estimated eight hundred Jews from the Nazis but resulted in the arrest and imprisonment of Corrie; her father, Casper; and sister, Betsie. Casper and Betsie died in the camps, but Corrie survived to tell their story.

Here are a few of Corrie's words about her experience in Ravensbruck taken from a letter she wrote in 1974. (Letter history can be found on endtimepilgrim.org.)

*We may have been the Lord's only representatives in that place of hatred, yet because of our presence there, things changed. Betsie and I, in the concentration camp, prayed that God would heal Betsie who was so weak and sick.*

*"Yes, the Lord will heal me," Betsie said with confidence. She died the next day, and I could not understand it. They laid her thin body on the concrete floor along with all the other corpses of the women who died that day. It was hard for me to understand, to believe that God had a purpose for all that. Yet, because of Betsie's death, today I am traveling the world telling people about Jesus.*

Corrie's message to her fellow prisoners is that "Jesus is Victor" and "There is no pit so deep that God's love is not deeper still." Speaking to a congregation in Africa destined for eventual martyrdom, Corrie told this story from her childhood as the congregants wondered fearfully if they would be next to die.

*"When I was a little girl," I said, "I went to my father and said, 'Daddy, I am afraid that I will never be strong enough to be a martyr for Jesus Christ.'"*

*"Tell me," said Father, "when you take a train trip to Amsterdam, when do I give you the money for the ticket? Three weeks before?"*

*"No, Daddy, you give me the money for the ticket just before we get on the train."*

*"That is right," my father said, "and so it is with God's strength. Our Father in Heaven knows when you will need the strength to be a martyr for Jesus Christ. He will supply all you need—just in time."*

~ 109 ~

Like Corrie Ten Boom, we are more than conquerors through Him that loved us. Tribulations are just another test. Although greater pressure may be applied, our leader always provides the possibility of release. The Christian in right relationship to God is not consumed by fear. What may cause your horse to run off a cliff won't get mine to bat an eyelash. What causes one person to slide into despair and depression may not cause the Christian to lose even an hour of sleep. Oswald Chambers said, "The saint never knows the joy of the Lord in spite of tribulation, but because of it." What a gift we have received.

The Christian lives in a completely different reality from the non-Christian. We are different. We are never abandoned to fend for ourselves once Christ has claimed us. One day that trailer will load up and head for home. As were the abandoned horses, many will be left watching as we head home, tucked securely into that trailer, destination heaven.

# CHANGED BY RELATIONSHIP

*For whom he foreknew, He also predestined to be conformed to the image of His Son. Moreover whom He predestined, these He also called; whom He called, these He also justified; and whom He justified, these He also glorified.*

Romans 8:29-30

*The individuality remains, but the mainspring, the ruling disposition, is radically altered. The same human body remains, but the old satanic right to myself is destroyed.*

Oswald Chambers

Each day is a new life, from the birth of morning and waking up to the death of evening and sleeping. We are made each day to come to God for our daily bread (Luke 11:3) whether the food is spiritual, mental, physical, or actual nourishment for our bodies. It was once said that if we live each day as if it were our last, one day we would most certainly be correct. Jesus cautions us not to worry about tomorrow; today is all we are guaranteed. Horses do not worry about whether the grass will still be green tomorrow or if the water barrel will still be filled. Are they wiser than we are?

Am I as faithful as Bo and Swizzle, indeed, all four of our horses? They have the safety and company of their small herd, yet each morning they eagerly await my coming. As I open their stall gates in turn, they come briskly—occasionally at a full gallop! They already have plenty of food and water; they have society; they have freedom, yet as soon as they see me, they come running. And not just in the mornings. No matter what the time of day, expected or not, if I appear bound for the barn, or anywhere they have access, the horses come. Especially Swizzle.

As our relationships deepen and my grays take on more of the mannerisms, habits, and behaviors that I teach them, they give up more and more natural freedoms. Or so it appears to the uninitiated. The test is always the same. Their obedience is only real if they have the opportunity to *not* obey. It is because they have a choice that I value their submission so greatly. Yet every day they choose more and more to stay at my side when freedom is just behind them in the open fields.

Why do Bo and Swizzle choose me over freedom? It can't be just food; they have food and water in the pasture. They choose me because they have begun to accept me as their leader, the source of safety, mental stimulation, entertainment, and affection. We have relationship.

It is easy for Bo and Swizzle to trust me to make the big decisions in life. It is comforting for them to know the rules and the security of boundaries. Horses are prey animals. I make them safe. Bo and Swizzle can "be still and know that I am."

**Be Still, and Know That I Am God**

Seeking Christians find many concepts of right relationship with God difficult to understand and even more difficult to apply in their lives. As a one-time seeker myself, I understand the mindset and bewilderment that goes with that territory. While I now consider myself found, I owe much of my enlightenment to my relationship with horses and the insights those relationships provide me. Psalm 46:10 is an oft-quoted verse that is profound and multi-layered and offers valuable insight and security to those who examine it with the simplicity of a child—or a horse. There are two distinct ways in which we can read this verse, two ways in which we can be comforted and strengthen our faith and relationship with God.

The first way is to read the verse as "Be still, and know that I am. (Signed) God."

This may be interpreted as "Rest... I am awake. (Signed) your Father." This is a message of safety and security. As a small child, did you ever awake suddenly from a sound sleep and were instantly afraid? Then you heard the quiet voices of your parents in the next room and realized you were not alone; you were protected and, greatly reassured, drifted peacefully back to sleep.

Victor Hugo, author of *Les Miserables*, tells us to, "Have courage for the great sorrows of life and patience for the small ones; and when you have laboriously accomplished your daily task, go to sleep in peace. God is awake."

The second manner in which we may interpret this verse is to read it as, "Be still! Know that I am God." This version may be understood as, "Be quiet and sit down! I will do what I say. You need only wait." This message is one of authority and promise. God is who He says He is, and He can do what He says He can do. We are not to worry about anything but our tasks of the day and maintaining a right relationship with him.

Bo and Swizzle look to me for their daily needs and in doing so take on more of the attributes of this new nature. Yet both completely retain their own personality. I delight in the nuances of each. Bo and Swizzle remain truly equine, yet distinctly different from the prey natures they began with.

Every horse has a unique personality, just as humans do. God delights in our uniqueness—to watch us become all He knows we can be, to maximize the possibilities of his design.

## The Error of Asking Why

Do Bo and Swizzle ever backslide? Yes, but not often. Each occurrence simply shows me where our relationship is not yet strong enough, where vulnerability and temptation lie. Usually, if I'm honest, the fault is mine for not devoting enough time and attention to our relationship. Bo and Swizzle are always ready; I'm the one who gets sidetracked by events in other areas of my life. For that matter, you may ask if I ever backslide in my relationship with God. Yes I do, and again, the fault is mine.

Whether due to arrogance or a lack of trust in God, I continue to find myself in error, the error of thinking independently of God and His direction. As is the case with my grays, these times prove a need to strengthen my relationship with the Lord. When once you are rightly related to God, you will no longer find yourself asking, "Why?" When you are addressing God and you begin with "why," you can pretty much bet you are in the wrong frame of mind or spirit. Immediately when we ask "why," we are in relational error with God. My horses are not to ask "why" as if I answered to them; they are to obey, trust, and be confident in my ability to provide leadership.

The question "why" in many cases may be translated as, "Give me your reasons, and I will decide if I agree with them." I do not intend to lead Bo and Swizzle by committee, and you may be certain God has a similar point of view. Each of us has a place (or places) where we find it difficult to simply trust in the Lord's plan without wanting to know why He does as He does. Where do you still ask why?

For example, everyone in North Texas received wonderful amounts of rain this past week. Some areas got way more than they wanted, and we got precious little. "Why," I asked yet again, "did the rain go north of us, or south of us, or miss us by what seems like inches to the west or east? Why is it becoming normal for rain to mysteriously evaporate only a mile or two before it gets here? Why don't we get the rain? Is it something we've done?"

Oops, perhaps that's the reason why. Rain, or more correctly, the lack thereof, is a recurrent issue where I am guilty of lack of trust in God. I know that I believe He will send the amount of rain we need; yet I have not been able to completely block out that nagging feeling of discontent or disappointment when the rain is so close yet passes by without blessing our pastures.

How easy it is to stray. Both intellectually and spiritually, I know that there is only one who can make it rain—or make it stop. God is on His throne, and I am blessed, so why could I not eliminate that little voice asking "why"? Did you catch that? I was asking "why" about "why." (Oh what tangled webs we weave…) Are we guilty of being most thankful for the blessings God bestows upon us, or are we most grateful for the relationship we share with Him? What a fine distinction there is between loyalty to what God says and loyalty to who He is. Will I ever master it? As the issue pertains to the question of rain, yes. The secret was to go cold turkey. I simply quit worrying about rain on the pastures. I have the tools and the responsibility to keep the lawn watered. However, I have zero ability to make it rain on the fields. Finally, after praying, I realized that I had not turned that problem over to God...not really. So I did. I am relieved to say that I just don't think about rain any longer. We have also had a lot more of it since I quit thinking about it.

Our consideration should not be for the circumstances we find ourselves in, but in finding out who God is. The blessing of relationship isn't provided through our familiarity with Scripture but through our familiarity with Him. We strive not to understand God but to obey Him. There comes a place in the relationship we enjoy with our horses where they have learned to trust and obey and no longer ask us why. For Bo and Swizzle, there is no level of advancement past that. For children of God, however, we will someday be privileged to understand the "whys" of all that we experienced in this earthly journey. We may not have all the answers on this side of eternity, but we may be confident that they will come.

**Self-Esteem**

Yesterday we trailered Swizzle and Copper over to a friend's property. Swizzle needs to be hauled; she needs to get away from her home environment and see more of the world. Many horse owners would think that this is a process of desensitization. Desensitization is exposing horses to different objects and environments so they learn not to be afraid of them. In a way, they are correct, but it is impossible to introduce every possible object, noise, and location to your horse. My purpose in hauling Swizzle is to test her trust in me. By placing her in a potentially stressful situation I can evaluate how well she focuses on me or whether she becomes distracted and fearful by the unfamiliar. My goal is to build Swizzle's confidence in me as her leader, so that regardless of object, place, or situation, she will be secure and look to me when she needs direction. I am working on short-circuiting her natural fight-or-flight response.

Confidence is only gained when we are tested and succeed. One of the great lies in our culture today is that self-esteem comes from a lack of failure. Wrong. Self-esteem is built by overcoming failure. Confidence and self-esteem come from the same foundation.

Our confidence in God does not grow because our circumstances are smooth and challenges are kept to a minimum; our confidence grows when we come to the end of our limits and fail, when God moves in to elevate us, to turn failure into success, to turn principle into faith.

## Working Out What He Works In

Everyone who has spent any time around preachers or reads Christian devotional material is familiar with the concept "working out what He works in." Be brutally honest with yourself. Do you really understand what it means? For many folks this idea is too abstract to allow them to apply it in their lives. We get close to putting the pieces together but miss nailing it completely. We believe that our salvation was purchased by the finished work of Christ on the cross, and we are now indwelt with the Holy Spirit. But now, how do we actually "work it out"?

Our salvation, our relationship with God is worked out through trial, error, correction, and success. We go through the trials, we make mistakes, God corrects us, and our obedience leads to success. The truth is that God loves us to the end of our disobedience and past it until we eventually achieve success. In 1 Corinthians 4:8, Paul tells us "we are hard-pressed on every side, yet not crushed; we are perplexed, but not in despair." We should expect, even welcome, trials to work through. As long as the lessons keep coming, we are still in His training program.

The first time I took Bo on a competitive trail ride I finally learned what "working out what is worked in" actually means. Bo began the ride in his usual way, soft and obedient. Bo had only been on one other big trail ride, but it was nothing compared to the natural obstacles we would encounter on this ride. The trail took us down narrow paths so steep they were nearly vertical, and I was practically lying down on Bo's back to give him a chance to balance as he gamely negotiated our descent safely. I was so proud of him.

Once you go down, it is a pretty good bet that you must go up at some point. So, up the next hillside we went, where the path was only rock and bits of shale between tall trees, the slippery stones tending to move as Bo carefully placed his feet on the loose material, picking his way in this unfamiliar environment. Instead of lying on Bo's back as we made our way up the steep hills, I now had a handful of mane right behind his ears and was lying along the top of his neck. It is seldom wise to allow green horses to make such a climb at anything faster than a walk, and I insisted Bo think his way along and up, at times having to nearly buck up the trail to gain momentum to get over the top and on to more level ground.

Bo was pretty good, getting just the tiniest bit fussy, until we reached the midpoint of the ride. Bo does not usually get fussy, so I knew we had strained our relationship, but I didn't realize how much. The middle of the ride passed the starting point and then continued in the opposite direction from which we began. That meant that we passed the area where all our trailers were parked when we left the rocky part of the ride and made a transition to the river part of the ride. Bo must have thought it was time to go back to the trailer because he was completely undone at the next obstacle. While we didn't have a wreck, the judge had to give us a score of zero on the obstacle. We didn't cause a scene, but Bo wasn't obedient either. The obstacle was one that he should have performed without bothering to twitch more than one ear. Bo was not soft and responsive, and I knew he was not "with" me any longer.

Shortly after the botched obstacle, we rode through a large pasture in which two parallel logs were placed, about thirty feet between the first and second logs. Please understand, Bo will jump, Bo does arena trail, and Bo will go over or through poles or logs on the ground no matter how they are configured. Bo got to the first log then stopped and snorted as if he expected it to suddenly open jaws and devour him. If you've ridden horses very much, you know just how far they can lean backwards when they do not wish to go forward. Their feet don't move, but in profile, they look like they're slipping backwards down a steep hill, neck and nose stretched way out and down in front of them. Bo absolutely refused to politely go over the logs.

Obedience had left the building. I dismounted, got out my lead rope, and snapped it to Bo's rope halter. I tied the reins through the swell of the saddle and proceeded to put Bo into a familiar exercise. I asked him to trot softly and politely in the direction I pointed and then stop and roll back over his hocks to go the opposite way when I asked. In this exercise, I seldom let a horse make a full circle around me; the goal is obedience, not fatigue. The lead rope is only eight or ten feet long, so a horse has to be really soft to perform this exercise well. It took a few minutes for Bo to "see" me again and decompress. I knew he wasn't back with me 100 percent, but time was wasting and Baber was waiting on us.

After remounting, Bo and I walked over the logs and off we went to the find the next obstacle. The trail continued to go up and down soft banks winding among low tree branches. Trees in our part of Texas aren't as tall as ones up north, so it was a pretty cramped path. The river would be coming up somewhere soon, and our directions were to enter the river, circle around markers out in the middle, and then return to the bank and continue on. I had little confidence that Bo would do the river obstacle well in his present frame of mind, but since he does love to play in water, I had some hope we would come to an understanding. I had never ridden Bo through water to this point and hoped for good footing and clear water.

As we came around and down the trail to where the trees finally opened enough to see ahead, we were only twenty feet from the water's edge. Only then did I get my first glimpse of the wide, mucky, suck-your-boots-off-sticky bank and muddy brown Paluxy River. The judge stood on dry land well away from the river when I asked him how deep the water was. He answered, "About belly or chest high on your horse." I figured I would give Bo one shot at it but not press the issue if he wasn't keen on the idea. There was no opportunity to work through a refusal, so I had no choice but to make only a minor request, and if I am honest, I really didn't want my saddle and boots getting completely trashed. Not surprisingly, Bo refused.

While I wasn't particularly saddened that we didn't get to enjoy the water feature, I was nonetheless disappointed in Bo's response. Our relationship is amazing because we are both committed to it. Bo's commitment seemed to be slipping and I began to consider my options as we continued the ride. We wound through the woods a bit longer before emerging into a clearing that led up to the final obstacle, the "Texas Vine." The vines hung from a horizontal pole suspended between two exceptionally large trees. Each vine was a rubber hose or plastic rope spaced about two inches apart. The obstacle required Bo to walk quietly through the curtain of "vines."

Approximately 150 feet before the vines we encountered four short landscape timbers arranged in a box on the grass, forming the outline of a small square about thirty inches across. I figured that walking Bo through the box should be a piece of cake and give me the opportunity to remind him that he knows how to do all these things. Well, as you may have already guessed, Bo did not walk through the box. He snorted and tried to slip around the box. Actually, I was a little taken aback. How could Bo and I have gotten so far off base in such a short time? And more importantly, what was I going to do about it? There could be no further "if" in Bo's response or I would deserve to lose my role of leader. Bo was not obedient, and I require obedience from him. I asked him repeatedly to walk through the box. Bo repeatedly offered to go around the box but would not go forward through it. Through the application and release of pressure, I told Bo that the only way he was going to move off that one spot, dead in front of the box, was to go forward through the box.

**A Line in the Sand**

My directions were given precisely and allowed no wiggle room. When Bo tried to move to the right he ran into my right leg. When he tried to escape to the left he ran into my left leg. When he tried to back up he ran into both my legs. Every door was closed to Bo but the one directly in front of him. Had you been sitting in a lawn chair with a glass of iced tea watching our exchange, you would not have seen anything particularly impressive. Bo didn't explode, and I didn't punish him. There was simply no option on earth other than Bo walking through the box. No matter what it took, I would keep with him until he worked it out.

Bo got the message. His body softened, he let out a deep sigh, and he very politely and confidently walked through the box as if he had done it daily since birth. Bo was back.

Directly ahead were the Texas Vines. I had a plan. Bo was instructed to walk confidently up toward the vines. When we were about ten feet away, I sat down, said whoa, and Bo obediently stopped. After a few seconds passed, I asked Bo to calmly walk forward again. He did. When only four feet separated his nose from the vines, I sat down again and Bo obediently stopped. The test came: I quietly asked Bo to go forward, and he did. Bo pushed his soft little gray nose through the vines and walked on as if they weren't even there.

Bo taught me what it means to "work out what he works in." Bo is my family. I have chosen him and Swizzle to be related to me as long as they live, and they have chosen me. There is nothing more important than the quality of our relationship. Bo never left the relationship, but his "nature" took over, resulting in his disobedience. I was not going to lose him. I loved Bo past his capacity to be disobedient. I was committed. Why did I not love Minnie enough to keep her from ending up at the pound? Because Minnie was not a chosen one. Minnie had every opportunity to enjoy a cushy life with a loving family. Minnie chose not to be related to me. I offered; she said, "No." I said, "Have it your way."

Bo went through trial, made errors, received correction, and achieved success. Bo and I were rightly related again, his old nature again put away. Every time he overcomes his old nature, our relationship strengthens. God sends us trials and challenges and allows us to commit to the error of disobedience. God's love will never be exhausted before we come to the end of our disobedience, resulting in an even greater and richer relationship than ever.

Jesus "loved his own who were in the world, he loved them to the end" (John 13:1).

## Disposable Relationships

Inexhaustible love is one characteristic unique to chosen relationships. No matter what, I will love Bo and Swizzle past any issues that arise; our relationships are not disposable. I might wager that 80 percent of marriages today would find both the bride and groom admitting, even as they prepared to exchange vows, that they were consciously entering into a disposable relationship. The marriage will last until one does something the other considers a deal breaker, or simply until a better opportunity comes along.

Just as inexhaustible love is a characteristic of chosen relationships, so is exceptional commitment. I do not allow any disobedience from Bo or Swizzle to go unanswered. To do so would be to fail as their leader. Leadership is not a part-time job; the commitment must be complete.

When you see parents who allow their young children to disobey their direction without consequence, you are seeing evidence of either a disposable relationship or a parent without adequate leadership skills. The parent or horse owner who fails to correct acts of disobedience are either *unable* to lead or *unwilling* to lead. If unwilling, the sad fact is that their horse or child is simply not important enough to them to do what is required to keep the relationship on healthy terms.

Chosen relationships are those between individuals that nothing can destroy. Both spirits are confident in the worth and nature of the other and have withstood the tests and trials of independence, success, failure, and the unexpected. Nothing on earth will change the commitment each has made to the relationship. How many of your relationships are chosen ones? How many are actually disposable? Let me repeat: in chosen relationships, both spirits have reason to be confident in the worth and nature of each other.

One might think that the parent-child relationship is a chosen one. Perhaps, but not necessarily. How many parents die while yet estranged from their children? We have all known parents who withdrew their love from their child for one reason or another. Similarly, children may withdraw love from a parent when some issue becomes more important than the relationship.

God knew us before we were born. Our relationship with Him is the sole exception I know of where a chosen relationship was created before relationship was consciously entered into. Perhaps we did know God before we were born, already committed to the relationship. All other relationships are built from the bottom up, from a first introduction or by birth into a family.

The extent to which we will go to preserve the relationships we choose for life is nearly, but not quite, limitless. A characteristic of disposable relationships is that the one in leadership works at guiding and correcting the follower until the work required exceeds any perceived benefit. When we allow disobedience or error to go completely uncorrected, we admit to being in a disposable relationship. There is a wide range of corrections, both by type and degree, which are employed as we build relationships with our followers. There also exists an unnatural relationship where the one in power is unbalanced or evil and will actually sacrifice the life of the follower in order to prevent a failure of relationship. An example of an unnatural relationship is the parent who murders his/her child in order to save it.

To fully understand the depth of commitment involved in chosen relationships, we have as the only pure example that of God and His children. As we learn in Romans, nothing can separate us from the love of God. There is no circumstance in which His chosen will be bounced from the training program or fail to find and pass through the narrow gate to freedom. God loves us past every trying circumstance, though He never guarantees us that the journey will always be easy. Much depends on how quickly we master the lessons presented along the way.

In the musical version of *Les Miserables*, the character Jean Val Jean reflects on his deathbed, "To love another person is to see the face of God." Jean Val Jean had a truly chosen relationship with his adopted daughter, Cosette. When you recognize the significance of the inexhaustible commitment you make in chosen loving relationship with another, you are blessed with the tiniest peek at God's face. I was blessed with one small glimpse on the trail with Bo as we approached the Texas Vines.

Some may ask, "What do I do when I have chosen a relationship but the other party has shut me out?" First, I must remind you that the relationships we are discussing here have already been proven to be worthy. However, there is only one way to address what are presently one-sided relationships. Imagine there is a bridge between you and the one you have committed to love no matter what. Midway across the bridge, the other individual has erected a barrier you cannot breach. She may pile more and more rubble on her side, making it even more difficult to cross back over the bridge. You cannot do anything to clear out her side of the bridge, but your resolve to keep your side of the bridge clear, swept, and spotless is evidence of your commitment. In the event the other individual decides to return to you, she need only get past her own junk before reaching the clean slate on your side of the bridge.

**Forever Changed**

I acknowledge no limit to the relationships I treasure with Bo and Swizzle. They are secure as my chosen grays. Through them I am blessed with a greater understanding of just how much my Father in heaven is committed to me. The greatest concept I was shown in the writing of this book is what chosen relationship truly means and that God will love me past anything I could ever come up with, no matter what.

Through relationship, my grays have radically altered the ruling disposition that is born into every prey animal. This change couldn't have happened without my influence as their leader and teacher. Like Bo and Swizzle, humans cannot have their sin nature radically altered without the work of Jesus Christ and the Holy Spirit. As children of God, the method by which we maximize the possibilities of our design is through the leadership and teaching God provides. Once we are chosen, God will never lose us. Throughout the rest of our lives we work out what He has worked in.

"I have learned to learn!" My own nature has been radically altered from the thoroughly sinful natural person I used to be through the persistent faithfulness of the Holy Spirit. The level of teamwork we have been able to achieve—His leadership and my obedient followership—is at a level I could never have imagined until I experienced it. Yet what level of training have I really reached? The summit? Hardly. I don't know if on a scale of one to ten I am at a one or an eight. Such evaluation will never be mine to make or to know. I am simply responsible for my daily tasks and to keep my focus on Jesus Christ.

What does more advanced training look like? First, I prove that I am, indeed, trainable. Once I have mastered elementary and secondary skill levels, my trainer becomes more confident that I have the heart and the desire to achieve more. Horses who achieve the highest levels of performance aren't always those with the most natural talent. One frequently sees a horse with more drive and more heart led by a faithful trainer win championships over horses with greater talent. Horses that learn how to learn and begin to love the process are the horses that can outperform a horse with extraordinary ability but no desire or little heart. My desire to be in relationship with Jesus Christ is a matter of heart, not aptitude.

**Practice Makes Perfect**

A 1996 research study by K.A. Ericsson studied the correlation between exceptional performance and deliberate practice. Every one of us has watched as a musician, athlete, or equestrian performs before an audience nearly frozen with awe and delight. This execution of amazing skill appears so effortless that we assume it is due mainly to special talent, and we may even consider such performers to be almost freaks of nature when we consider the level of excellence they have been able to achieve. The results of this research proved that the number one influence on achievement level for exceptional performers was the number of hours spent in solitary practice of their specific skill. The most exceptional musicians spent approximately ten thousand hours in practice, the lesser-accomplished professionals about five thousand hours, and the serious amateurs about two thousand hours. The study concluded

AMAZING GRAYS, AMAZING GRACE

that the accumulated amount of deliberate practice is closely related to the attained level of performance.

I believe this finding is as true in relationships as it is for performers. Do you think saints are made quickly? Is that amazing horse so attuned with its rider by accident or luck? Deliberate practice with your horse yields higher levels of performance. Likewise, time spent in the tutelage of the Spirit creates greater obedience and relationship with God.

As I learned to learn, my Trainer has helped me achieve smaller goals of task and obedience. I love the process. With each new concept my Trainer presents, it becomes easier for me to understand the next. The obedience I bring, led by the skill of my Trainer, creates a synergy of relationship that allows me to continue to master new and more complicated obstacles and maneuvers.

Do I know what my Trainer has in mind for a final goal? I have no idea, yet I am confident I will be safely kept until my work is done. At the end of my productive life, I will be lovingly retired to a home created just for me, yet I will continue in relationship.

**Live in the Present**

As Bo learns to softly assume different body frames, right posture then left, left posture then right, half-pass, shoulder in, does he worry about why he is learning these skills? Does he ask why? No, which is a primary reason why he, like so many other wonderful horses, is amazing. How many people can be obedient without asking why or sulling up until they reach agreement with the program? How many horses?

Our job is to learn what God has to teach us today, not to lament over what we missed yesterday or worry

~ 128 ~

about what we will see tomorrow. We are to be obedient and to softly and happily yield to His pressure. Let Him lead. How silly, and perhaps self-destructive to the process itself, worrying about what each lesson means. Bo cannot understand the plans I have for his future. Neither can we begin to grasp what God's plan is for each of us.

Having learned to learn, I am happy and content in the daily process. Some tasks are more difficult to learn than others, and I just keep trying until the puzzles are solved. It is a long road to accumulate ten thousand hours of deliberate practice, but I am dedicated to the pursuit of excellence. If you are faithful to practice every day, some day you will be exceptional.

At the end of every lesson, Bo knows I will groom him and rub any muscle that was overly taxed as he successfully worked through his exercise. I will leave him snug and comfortable in his stall with fresh hay and bedding or turn him out to play in the warm sunshine of his pasture to nibble grass or simply nap. I know that at the end of each day the Lord will be there as I snuggle deep under my covers without a care, because I know that He does not sleep.

"Be still and know that I am God."

Good night, Father  Good night, Bo.

# IT'S NOT THE HORSE, IT'S THE RELATIONSHIP

*If you love Me, you will keep my commandments.*

John 14:15

*A beautiful saint may be a hindrance if he does not present Jesus Christ, but only what Christ has done for him; he will leave the impression—"What a fine character that man is!"—that is not being a true friend of the Bridegroom (John 3:29). We have to be more careful of our moral and vital relationship to Him than of any other thing, even of obedience.*

Oswald Chambers

Regularly people say to Baber or me, "Oh, if only I had a horse like Bo. You are so lucky." Others may ask if he is for sale; they want what I have. The truth is they don't want Bo per se; they want a relationship with their horse like I have with Bo. Just as it is wrong to admire the character of that beautiful saint Chambers refers to rather than the work of Jesus Christ, which initiated and directed their relationship, so it is incorrect to identify Bo as the special thing desired. What others desire is the relationship that as his trainer I initiated and directed with Bo, made special by the commitment he has also made to relationship.

~ 131 ~

Have you ever looked at a father and son who were so obviously connected to each other that you wished you could have had a father like him or that your son would be like this one? We may think, *What a different path my life would have taken if I had a parent like that one.* When you see a long-married couple still holding hands after fifty years of laughter and heartbreak, so obviously in love with each other that the line between them is but a blur, do you lament that you weren't blessed with a husband like him or a wife like her? How lucky they are. Why wasn't I as fortunate?

It may be an easier path for parents and their children to build strong bonds when they have been blessed with great role models. If your parents taught you how to be both humble and strong, you have far better odds of success raising your own children. Whether you look for that great spouse, wonderful children, or a horse like Bo, in each instance what you long for is not the person or the horse, but the special relationship you have witnessed.

The basics of building a special relationship between horse and trainer apply to creating successful relationships with children, in marriage, friendships, with teachers and their students, and any other relationships you pursue. You are better able to appreciate the possibilities of great relationships by observing the remarkable relationships others share. The most important relationship, of course, which serves as the cornerstone of all others, is the relationship you have with Jesus Christ.

**Lessons in Leadership**

Understanding relationships is not a simple matter. The concepts that apply to relationships are like most others we learn throughout our lifetimes. They are only mysteries until the moment when the light bulb of understanding begins to glow. How do we find the right partners for relationships? How do we build proper and strong foundations? How do we move from concentration on stuff and self and move to having eyes only for Jesus Christ? Like anything else, the journey begins with the first step. Chapter six of the book of Matthew is a great primer for beginners as well as a wonderful reminder for those already well into the relationship process.

In Matthew 6, Jesus gives us a wonderfully objective list of behaviors we are to do and behaviors we are not to do. Jesus gives us masterful lessons in charity and hypocrisy, showing us how charitable deeds done before men have their reward here and now and, therefore, earn no future reward from our Father in heaven. Verse 3 in chapter 6, however, is one of those mysteries that we are only able to unravel as our relationship with Jesus grows and matures.

*But when you do a charitable deed, do not let your left hand know what your right hand is doing.*

Matthew 6:3

A relationship with God has built-in prerequisites similar to those we encounter in higher education. Students are unable to understand more complex material without first learning the basics and building a foundation of knowledge. The example that comes to my mind immediately is technology. I have no relevant foundation, so there is no point trying to teach me how to construct a computer generated holographic image when it took me two and a half hours and a phone call to the manufacturer just to install my wireless mouse. Talk technology to me and my eyes glaze over.

How do we begin to build foundation and grow our relationship with Jesus Christ? Through His Word. And how are we to pray? The Lord's Prayer is found in the sixth chapter of Matthew. When all else fails, this prayer covers all the issues you will encounter in life. Are you concerned that you just aren't prepared, that you don't have enough foundation? In this same chapter, Jesus also talks about the futility of worry. As you consider the process of building a right relationship with God, I encourage you to concentrate on Jesus' lessons in Matthew 6.

As you progress in a relationship you will begin to understand why concentration on anything other than the relationship itself is but a distraction. You will begin to understand Matthew 6:3, when your actions begin to be generated by the relationship you share with Jesus Christ and not by conscious thought, debate, or intent. The charitable deed described in verse 3 is done unconsciously, just like breathing. It is an automatic action, not a calculated deed. The doing of charitable deeds becomes so familiar that we don't realize we have even done one. This automatic response begins by building habits of task and progresses until the mastery of tasks is replaced with the habit of obedience. When habit of obedience is reached, the limit of what is possible in a relationship expands to presently unknowable levels.

The relationship I have with Bo, when noticed by other horse owners, initiates conversation about our horses. Those conversations are my best opportunity to influence the future success of the relationship the inquiring horse owner has with his or her own horse. If I were to call a meeting to share my relationship testimony using words alone, there might be precious little benefit to anyone. The most important step in sharing my story is the notice and subsequent inquiry of the observer. The cliché, "a picture is worth a thousand words," is true in testimony. What is seen has a far greater impact than what is preached, and what is seen of us must always live up to what we preach.

Until I learned this lesson, I was always unsure of how I could possibly present Christ to another person. It seemed all the other Christians knew how to share. I did not. My grays are the key to my understanding that all I need do is present the benefits of this chosen relationship to seekers who inquire. I've been doing that for many years with people who look for better results with their horses. It is not "me" that causes a person to inquire about my security, joy, peace, and success. It is not *my* security, joy, peace, or success they want. What they want is their own relationship with Jesus Christ. Bo is not special in any way their horse is not. I am not special in any way they are not. What is special is the relationship I share with Bo and my relationship with Jesus.

No great relationships happen by accident or luck.

Who has most positively influenced your life? Was it a person who stood upon a stage and gave you a laundry list of things to do? Did you really get your money's worth from that expensive set of tapes telling you how to achieve happiness or wealth with little to no effort? Or have you been most greatly blessed by the people who are simple and authentic in their speech, manner, and message?

**Once-in-a-Lifetime Relationships**

Is there just one perfect horse in a lifetime? I don't think so. The method for producing these seemingly once-in-a-lifetime relationships is formulaic in a way. When the right trainer and the right horse get together, there is still the necessity of commitment, time, maintenance, leadership, obedience, correction, and building confidence in the relationship. However, once trainers are properly educated and experienced, they may only have enough time and energy remaining in their career to forge just one such relationship. These relationships take years to develop and mature, just like the marvelous relationship of that long-married couple mentioned at the beginning of this chapter.

Not surprisingly, great horse trainers usually make their living training horses. They begin each morning riding client's horses and continue through the day until all their work is done. In case you didn't know, the best trainers ride more than ten head per day, sometimes many more than ten per day. Assistant trainers or apprentices work others until each horse reaches a stage where only the trainer can refine and advance the horse's level of performance. As you can imagine, little if any time remains to build relationships with the trainer's own horses. The horse trainer's business is to train and sell, train and sell.

There were years I actually looked forward to brushing a tail or cleaning a stall. All "my" horses had a closer personal relationship with my assistant trainer than they had with me. Rodolfo groomed them, bathed them, talked with them, and usually emptied the feed buckets into their stall feeders. The horses didn't know (and didn't care) that I had personally prepared each bucket, often changing the content and amount daily for the younger horses. During the working day, Rodolfo would hand me a horse and I would teach the lesson. Afterwards, I handed the finished horse back to Rodolfo and started the next. Was I a good leader? I certainly tried. Was I building relationship? Yes, but not like I have with my grays today.

As you have probably discovered by now, I am a believer in relationships. I have some natural ability as a horse trainer, but the desire, the heart, the relationship I built with each horse in my training barn is what allowed me to do my best work. There were times I wondered why I didn't have the degree of success with all horses that I had with some of them. In most instances I was confident of the responses I would get from each horse in a competitive situation. However, there were other horses I only had a pretty good idea of what they were likely to do. Consistency was not king. The reason for the difference between confidence and hopefulness was relationship.

## No Time Equals No Relationship

Relationships thrive on commitment. Close relationships require daily time spent together. If I don't spend time with Bo and Swizzle nearly every day, other relationships will become more important to them and those other relationships will strengthen as ours weakens. If all their time is spent with the herd, or simply with each other, my role diminishes. Bo and Swizzle will get what they need elsewhere.

The same is true with our relationship with Jesus Christ. He is ever faithful to the demands of a daily relationship. Are you? Do you make it a priority to seek Him daily, to strengthen your relationship? If not, other relationships will strengthen with friends, family, video games, etc., and yours with Him will weaken. Relationships take time. It became popular in the 1970s and '80s for parents to use quality time as an excuse for not giving much quantity time to their children. How misguided we were. Is there really such a thing as quality time? Sure, but there is a catch. Quality time is a judgment of worth, not a time frame. It is a misuse of the term itself and rather like propaganda (rationalization) to use the term *quality time* to define short, content-laden time rather than time that teaches or reinforces relationship foundations of task, confidence, and affection.

The best way to produce a great horse is using the wet saddle blanket method. There is an old joke about a greenhorn rider who was advised to use this technique to gentle his unruly horse. Days later the greenhorn returned to the old hand and said, "I got that old saddle blanket plumb dripping before I put it on old Brownie—it didn't help at all." Of course, a wet saddle blanket is one that starts out nice and dry but becomes thoroughly saturated with horse sweat during long working sessions. Repeating the wet-saddle-blanket exercise makes great horses. Trying to cheat the time commitment required reduces the probability of building strong relationships. The only way to define quality time is by the fruit—the result of time spent together. Quality time always produces stronger relationships. The greater the quality and quantity of time, the greater the strength of the relationship.

Can we ever spend short periods of time with horses, children, or Jesus Christ that are meaningful? Absolutely. But they are meaningful only if they reinforce what was previously established during the longer periods of time spent together building a relationship.

**Strangers in the House**

Many parents today are shocked when they discover what their children have been doing with their time. You hear stories on the nightly news documenting the often-tragic results of a parent-child relationship that left the kids basically adrift in the world without supervision, values, limits, and security. If they were committed to relationship with their children, parents wouldn't be surprised to find their child is involved in robbery, sex games, drugs, or worse. Such parents may be exhausted from work, housekeeping, friendships, athletic pursuits, school, whatever—maybe even church activities. If you spend most of your time as a parent organizing and managing your children's schedule, watch out. You are no longer mom and dad; you have become the kid's activities coordinator. You have sacrificed your relationship with your children and created a situation where the kids have no choice but to build other relationships outside the family.

In strong, secure relationships there is no substitute for time spent together. Bi-coastal marriages generally fail because all the important relationships exclude the other spouse. You cannot have a great marriage unless it is the one relationship that receives more of your concentration than any other, save your relationship with God. Your children are little more than resident strangers unless they spend a significant amount of their time with you. You will not have the relationship with Jesus Christ you desire without making the attendant time commitment.

Once our important relationships are established, they require ongoing maintenance. Relationships with other people require maintenance no less than the one we have with our horse. The quantity of time we spend in our various relationships defines the quality of the relationship. You are free to think otherwise, of course, but an objective evaluation of where you spend your time and the fruits of each relationship will tell the real story.

Maintenance interludes may be conducted quickly. Some days if I have little time to spend with Bo and Swizzle, I may just hop on bareback with a halter and play walk-trot trail in the arena. We do lots of standing around; I lie down on their backs and watch the clouds drift across the sky; I hug their necks; we fortify our relationships. By sandwiching a few maneuvers between these affection sessions, I reinforce the habit of obedience. We reinforce what is already mastered. Never introduce anything new when you have limited time. It never fails—if you rush out to do a twenty-minute drill on your horse, there is a law somewhere that requires your horse to contradict you or become confused. When that happens, you have no other responsible choice but to work through the issue until it is resolved. Your twenty-minute quickie drill has become an hour and a half lesson.

When a bareback ride is just not possible, I may take just a few moments to brush, pet, hug, and maybe offer a horse cookie. I feed cookies and carrots every once in a while. Carrots are usually reserved for birthdays and trips away from home when I want to be sure my horses get adequate hydration. Carrots contain lots of water, and I feed them on hot days as my horses stand tied to the trailer at an event.

**Elements of Relationship**

These quick visits may be considered quality time. However, they are only effective if used infrequently. All the time I spend with Bo and Swizzle builds up savings accounts of relationship. Time apart from them makes withdrawals from those accounts. Short maintenance visits do not change the balance in the account one way or the other, but only for that one day. We must be careful to make significant, regular deposits to our relationship accounts or we will find that the balance begins to decline.

Security in relationships comes from clarity, consistency, transparency, and accountability. Roles and rules must be absolutely clear. Rules and boundaries are to be fixed and never violated without consequence. This consistency is arguably the most important component of our relationships, though none of these elements will be effective in the absence of the others. Roles, actions, and consequences must all be transparent. As is the case with humans, in our relationship with our horse, directions and expectations must easily be understood or the horse will become confused, inconsistent in response, and insecure in the relationship. Accountability is an aspect of relationships seen less and less frequently in western societies today. Fewer great trainer-horse relationships exist, fewer great marriages exist, fewer great children are being raised, and fewer proper relationships between God and men exist today.

This lack of accountability is one of the greatest contributing factors to weak or failed relationships. When accountability is absent, we become insecure, one result being poor self-esteem. When we are not held accountable for our decisions and behavior, what is our motivation to conduct ourselves well? Bad behavior in horses goes undisciplined mostly because the responsible humans don't understand horse language and don't recognize rude, and potentially dangerous, behavior. The only other possibility is the humans just don't care enough to do the work necessary to provide consistent leadership. The end result is the same: either the horse or human being injured, or the horse is condemned as bad and discarded or passed on to someone else. Do you see the similarity with many of our youth today?

Few people are held accountable today. Small wonder so many relationships, economies, and governments fail. Businesses and individuals don't live up to their advertising, promises, or their responsibilities; and yet there is no consequence for the lack of performance. Do you think our relationship with God is the exception to this present absence of accountability? It is not. We may attempt to rationalize our way out of the responsibility for poor decision-making or try to shift the blame to someone else (all the rage today), but we will still be held accountable. God is not mocked; He is not fooled, and we can ride the lie we tell ourselves all the way to our final disastrous destination.

## Mere Belief Does Not Create Truth

Sometimes truth hurts. There is no pleasant way to describe sin. Choosing to label sin a bad choice is the politically acceptable way of saying, "Give me a pass." Perhaps you can find others who will buy this line. I guarantee you God will not. You are accountable. Consider the fifteenth century explorers who all believed the world was flat. All those sailors whose names we learned in grammar school history and geography class agreed the world was flat; all the maps said so too. No matter how strong this belief was or how widespread the agreement among men, the earth was not flat. It still isn't last I checked.

What's true is true. Holding a belief to the contrary is simply error. Greater belief or greater agreement will not make what is not true any less false. If you ever need a reality check regarding accountability, start working with horses. Horses give you absolutely honest feedback about your behavior. They do not accept false rationalization. You must bring true leadership and the responsibility that goes with it or the horse will ignore you, hurt you, or leave you when given the opportunity. People who are selling the fallacy of equality without accountability are either misguided or liars; in either case, they would be complete failures as horse trainers.

Some horses will put up with more bad behavior from humans than others, but eventually they will all have enough of the irritating human and do whatever it takes to leave the scene or physically challenge the human. I usually take the horse's side, of course. Horses do not rationalize. Horses understand that there are horses lower on the pecking order and higher on the pecking order than they. The horse that achieves a leadership role in the herd also accepts responsibility. If the lead horse fails to be accountable, they lose their leadership role and the herd itself may be placed in danger. Isn't it odd how horses frequently appear to be more insightful and scriptural than humans?

Bo and Swizzle expect my requests or instructions to be clear and consistent; if they are not, I have demonstrated a failure in leadership. I am accountable to be a leader deserving of their followership. When I make a request of my horse and he gives me an incorrect response, I will always take action. If the horse is unable to comply, it is my responsibility to make him able. If the horse is unwilling to comply with my request, I am ready to make him willing. Horses are as accountable for making wrong choices as I am. The choice the horse makes, and understanding why he made it, determines the action I take in response.

Think about your relationships. The ones you value most are those where you understand your role, you have confidence in the consistency of response from the one you are relating to, and you know that you will be held accountable if you fall short in holding up your end. As trust, security, and affection build within a relationship, it moves from one of acquaintance to one of friendship and perhaps more. God is faithful. God never changes. God is consistent. We may have total confidence and security in His instruction and evaluation of us. His Word is clear, consistent, and transparent on this issue. He requires obedience, and we are accountable to Him—just as we are accountable to one another.

# THE DIFFERENCE BETWEEN LOVE AND LOVING LEADERSHIP

*Love is patient...it rejoices in the truth. Love never fails. When I became a man, I put away childish things.*

1 Corinthians 13:4, 6, 8, 11

*In the New Testament, love is more a verb than a noun. It has more to do with acting than with feeling. The call to love is not so much a call to a certain state of feeling as it is to a quality of action.*

Dr. R.C. Sproul

The message in Scripture is always one of relationship. At issue is our right relationship to God the Father, Jesus Christ the Son, and the Holy Spirit. My message throughout this collection is also one of right relationships: your relationship with your horse and what it teaches you about your relationship with God.

As Bo and Swizzle become more firmly committed to their relationships with me they become more rooted and grounded in my leadership. As prey animals, their nature was to be alert and fearful of nearly everything that moved suddenly or made an unexpected noise. Their relationship to me, and their confidence in my ability as a leader, has produced a change in their nature. As long as our relationships remain clear and strong, we will stay on course to a destination where Bo and Swizzle will eventually be fearless as leadership and relationship guides their new natures.

As Christians, we too have to be shaken out of everything that awakens fear till we also become fearless. This is evidence of a right relationship with Jesus Christ. As our faith and understanding in the nature of our almighty God grows, we ultimately arrive at a place where we fear nothing and no one. Can this same release from all fear be achieved by mere affection, or even love? Your own personal history and experience proves otherwise. Did your parents love you? If so, are you completely without fear? No, you aren't. If you are married, does your spouse love you unconditionally? Praise God if you can truthfully answer yes, but are you completely without fear? No, you aren't.

Is Jesus Christ your personal Savior? Are you a chosen child of the God of the Bible? If you answered yes to these questions, you are on a journey of relationship that will eventually remove all fear and worry from your life.

**My Daddy's Bigger Than Yours**

In their innocence, young children may be devoid of fear because they believe absolutely in the omnipotence of their parents. The young boy tells his neighborhood bully in complete confidence, "My daddy's bigger than your daddy." The child has no fear because he believes his father to be the biggest and greatest of all humans, without flaw or blemish.

Horses seldom progress in their emotional development and discernment past the level of prepubescent children. Many horses never make it out of the terrible twos. Until the little boy discovers his father is just a human with feet of clay he retains faith in the absolute excellence of his daddy. Ultimately every parent will topple from the pedestal their children place them upon. As the little boy begins to mature, he will begin to realize that Dad is just a man, regardless of how much love there is between father and son. The young man will also learn fear as he begins to see the world and other humans with a larger vision and awareness.

My goal with Bo and Swizzle is to continue adding to the breadth and height of the pedestal I've told them I stand upon. In the beginning I proved to them that I was indeed on a pedestal, but only an inch above the ground. The surface of that first pedestal was small—just big enough to include my personal space. Horses learn early that they are not to get within touching distance of me without an invitation. I pet them, I hug them, but the horse is not to initiate contact. Respect the pedestal.

As days, weeks, and years pass, the pedestal base enlarges in direct correlation to the depth and breadth of the relationship that exists between the horse and me. The physical space doesn't increase, but as the leader, I am given greater respect and earn more trust as the height of my pedestal rises.

So it is with children of God when once we come to faith that our God is the only God, the almighty God, the God of creation, the God who spoke the world into existence, and the God who is who He says He is and can do what He says He can do. Armed with this faith and our relationship with our awesome God, we no longer have any fear. God is a father bigger than any other. He is the one who will never fall from His throne. His feet are not made of clay.

There are horse owners who have wonderful, loving relationships with their horses. Their horses are comfortable with touch; their horses are willing, eager, participants in the relationship. The horses may hold their humans in high esteem, seeking out and finding real pleasure in their owner's company. And all may be well until the horse becomes afraid, or for that matter, the human exhibits fear.

Yes, your horse may love you, but as an equal. This is a great thing until trouble arrives. Many people are injured each year by their adoring horse. In normal circumstances this friendly horse would never cause its owner injury. The horse may even love the human. But when fear takes over, the flight instinct kicks in and that half-ton of muscle and bone will be on the move. Many a beloved owner has been trampled in that moment of panic.

**Who Do You Run to?**

When a human trainer is firmly established on a leadership pedestal her horse will not default to a fear mode. Right relationship with the trainer has actually changed the horse's nature. When unsure about a sound, movement, or situation the horse will immediately focus on the trainer to look for any sign of uncertainty or fear. Finding neither, the horse will ask, "What's the plan?" The trainers who deserve the leadership pedestal they claimed will always have a plan ready and give either direction or assurance to the horse as the situation warrants. Horses in strong relationship to their trainer, when confronted by fear, run *to* their trainer, not away from their trainer.

Christians, too, are blessed with a new nature. Things that create fear and concern in most people will regularly come to the notice of Christians. Christians, however, do not default into fear. We look to God on His throne for any sign of uncertainty or indecision. There will be none. As does the horse with faith in a worthy leader the Christian will ask for direction or bask in the complete assurance that God has a plan at the ready; His plan is perfect, and we are safe. When in doubt, Christians run to Jesus for safety.

Love may be grand, but loving leadership is the relationship that creates confidence, strength, defines our character, and allows us to enjoy perfect green pastures beside still, beautiful waters without any concern about potential dangers lurking just over the quiet hillside. God is on His throne. He has told us He is God. He has proven that He is God. We are secure.

What a wonder of grace is the gift of a right relationship with Jesus Christ. What a wonder of grace is the gift of relationship with my grays.

Three year-old Swizzle

# YOU CAN'T FOOL GOD

*O Lord, you have searched me and know me. For there is not one word on my tongue, but behold, O Lord, you know it altogether."*

Psalm 139: 1, 3

*Conscience is that faculty in me which attaches itself to the highest that I know, and tells me what the highest I know demands that I do. It is the eye of the soul which looks out either toward God or toward what it regards as the highest, and therefore conscience records differently in different people.*

Oswald Chambers

Are you really obedient? Is there a truth in the Bible that creates resistance in you the instant you read it? Such a reaction is normal for humans and proof that we still respond to the matter carnally, not spiritually. We deceive ourselves when we avoid issues we know have yet to be conquered or resolved. These are the areas in which we are not obedient. We do not follow the Lord's lead—and the reason is not inability, though many will wrongfully make that excuse. The reason is unwillingness. Pure and simple, we decide not to obey.

As the crafty humans we are, we often try to avoid difficult issues completely by pretending they don't exist. If we never open the door, who would ever know that we would refuse to walk through? Let me show you what happens in a similar scenario from the trainer-horse perspective.

Some trainers also avoid putting themselves and their horses in positions where they know the horse will absolutely refuse to comply with their request. Let's consider a horse that has a hissy fit whenever a rider touches it with a spur. We're not talking about the normal reaction a horse may have when first introduced to the spur that, if done correctly, is mild, of short duration, and is followed quickly by acceptance and understanding. A spur used properly is simply a means of more refined communication.

A spur should never be used in anger or frustration. I have known a number of trainers and riders who say their horse will not accept a spur and therefore they do not use them. I have ridden horses that didn't particularly care for spurs and some who didn't need them since they were already very responsive to small cues. However, I never let a horse tell me I could not use a spur. That would be admitting there was a door I was not allowed to open. To leave the door closed, avoid it and pretend it wasn't there proves a deficit in leadership, a place where the led becomes the leader. This is the beginning of a bigger wreck waiting somewhere down the road.

When a Christians purposefully avoids that one truth in the Bible that causes him to sull up in stubbornness, defiance, or just plain pissiness, it is evidence of a grab for the leadership role. God won't yield the day. He is too faithful. He knows that letting us have our way will only lead to a bigger wreck on another day.

## What to do when your horse tells you, "I don't do spurs!"

First you must be certain the case is one of refusal (unwillingness) and not one of inability due to poor foundation or lack of understanding. If the horse is unable to comply the good trainer will supply the foundation or education that will make it able.

If the horse in unwilling, the trainer must determine what caused the unwillingness and find a way to create willingness. Many times trainers don't know what a horse experienced in its past that created the problem behavior or reaction they are faced with today. If the trainer knows why the horse refuses it may make it easier to create a plan for change. But knowing the why isn't really necessary. The behavior or refusal can usually be fixed regardless of its origin.

Christians are subject to the same rules. Are we unwilling or unable to walk through that door we are avoiding? We can only answer this question by walking up to the door, opening it, and attempting to walk through. When a horse tells me that bad things will happen if I attempt to use a spur I must open that door and try to go through it. As a worthy leader I have to approach the door with a carefully prepared lesson plan. Before using spurs on such a horse I would work on very basic exercises to establish a dialogue. My training method is built upon a three-step system of communication.

The method is the same for many problems; I'm just using spurs as an illustration of the concept.

## Suggest. Request. Insist.

My training plan uses a simple 3-step rule. First I will suggest a response to the horse. If the mere suggestion doesn't produce the desired reaction then I specifically ask the horse to comply with my direction. If the direct request doesn't work I have to figure out the reason for the failure. Was my horse unable or unwilling? If the horse is unable to respond appropriately I provide additional instruction until it is able. If the horse is unwilling to do whatever maneuver I requested, I go to the third step: I *insist* the horse do as I ask.

Here's the 3-step method from a mother - son point of view. One afternoon Mom walks into the living room and finds her teenage son sprawled on the sofa playing video games. On her way down the hall she can't miss how messy his room is. Mom's goal is for her son to clean his room. She suggests, "I noticed your room needs to be straightened up." She looks at him - he meets her eye. Message delivered; Mom continues on her way to the kitchen.

Fifteen minutes later Mom comes back to the living room. Her son's feet have not moved. The suggestion did not work. She makes a direct request, "Please go clean your room." Again, eyes meet in understanding but the kid is not getting up off the couch. The request failed.

Is there anything that makes the boy unable to get up? Nope. So Mom escalates to the third step - insist. As a wise mother she knows exactly what is needed to get the kid up and start his feet moving swiftly in the direction of his room. Having been consistently "trained" the son realizes nothing else in life is going to happen until he cleans his room.

The key is consistency. On most occasions her son would immediately move his feet and go clean his room at his mother's suggestion alone. Relationship isn't static, training is never cast in stone, and Mom's faithfulness to always step in maintains her son's level of obedience.

Training a horse also requires consistency, faithfulness, and following through the entire 3-step process until feet move every single time.

Once I have established a leadership position with the horse, however tenuous, I increase the difficulty of maneuvers we perform until the horse gains confidence that I am fair and capable of leading him. Once we pass this point I ask the horse for a maneuver he has already performed successfully using the spur as part of my communication. At this point I want to see how the horse reacts to the spur and judge it within a very structured context. I am diagnosing the situation using the scientific method. Since only one variable changed from the maneuver we just did well I know that any resistance on the horse's part is a result of the difference. In this exercise the variable that changed was the addition of the spur.

As with any training issue, whether between God and man or trainer and horse there must be a plan. God's plan is always relevant, proper, and perfect. There is no response we can make to His pressure or communication that He isn't already three steps ahead of us. He always knows the range of possible reactions we might give and is prepared in advance to respond instantly with His next move. I call this "The Dance." He leads, we respond. Depending on our response, He leads again. And so it continues.

**Take Smaller Steps**

Once we determine that the issue isn't "I can't" but "I won't!" the worthy trainer will break down the door of unwillingness. A trainer can continue to pretend that the door isn't there but the horse will not be fooled and the relationship will be damaged. Refusing to approach a problem or pretend it isn't there is just playacting, trying to sell our refusal as innocence rather than disobedience. God certainly won't be fooled. Indeed, we are the fools.

What do we do with a horse that doesn't willingly accept the touch of a spur? As with any horse or human training program, we begin by breaking the process down into the most basic steps possible. If we encounter resistance at any point along the way there is always a smaller step possible. The process of breaking a task down into steps is like the math theorem—between any two points there is always another point.

Let's work through this spur issue beginning with a very basic step. From the ground, using a rope halter and lead, I would work the horse through a variety of bending and yielding exercises. This process establishes the most basic of foundations for horses that are easy to halter. By mastering these exercises, the horse learns respect, trust, confidence, accountability, and obedience. Once these basics are completed well, I might take a stiff riding crop and rub the horse with it all over its body. If you do not know how to quickly and quietly do these little exercises don't even try to address the actual issue of spur resistance.

Once trainer and horse are in tune and "dancing"—pressure, yield, pressure, yield—we can take the handle end of the crop, lightly place it on the horse's side where your spur normally touches, and ask him to move away from the pressure. Patience becomes the most important tool a trainer can have. If the horse leans into the handle of the crop (and at first they all do), continue to hold it firm. As soon as the horse even thinks about moving away release the pressure and remove the crop from the horse's side. Timing is key.

Rub the horse a few times with the crop on the withers and croup to show the horse that the crop itself has no particular power or threat. Only when the horse is calm and quiet will I use the crop to apply pressure to the horse's side again. Repeat this sequence until the horse moves easily and lightly away as soon as the crop handle touches his side. Now do the other side. We are testing to determine the source of the reaction to spur pressure. Where is it triggered? Eventually the horse will obediently accept the pressure on his side and move away from it softly. This is the exact response we want from our spur when we are riding the horse.

**Build Confidence**

Once the groundwork is successfully completed it is time to mount up and work our way through that resistant door. The process is the same. Back to basics; suggest, request, and insist on soft obedience. The good trainer will start the horse in an easy exercise like a figure eight at the walk. Show the horse the pattern and work through it a number of times until the horse knows exactly what is expected of him. This is how we build the horse's confidence.

Change the posture (frame) of the horse and continue the figure eight at an easy jog, preferably by changing seat and leg aids, making the transition from one direction to the other. If the horse isn't absolutely happy with the increase in speed return to the walk and begin again.

Reins are used only when absolutely necessary to offer a hint to the horse that his response isn't quite right. When the horse is responding properly to leg pressure in the circles and through the middle it is time to add the spur. Our leg will actually become lighter as we apply the spur to the horse's side. If we have done our job well, there will probably be very little response. This is the beginning of clearing the blockage that kept us from going through that door. By working a plan patiently, wisely, and consistently, the trainer and horse build confidence in each other and strengthen the relationship already created.

Whenever you leave a hole in the foundational training of a horse it will always come back to bite you later, and never at a convenient time. At some point the deficit will prevent you from acquiring a higher skill or limit the level of obedience and confidence your horse is able to offer. No issue has ever been repaired or resolved by ignoring it. The work must be done sooner or later. A good trainer knows this. There is no fooling the horse.

Do you think God is fooled when you try to ignore that one thing you are unwilling to acknowledge? We only deceive ourselves. The work must be done sooner or later. The door must be opened. We will never get a pass; the bill will become due and payable. It is easier to learn our lessons in a natural order of progression than to wait until a foundational weakness shows up at the worst possible moment. Where are you unwilling? Where do you think you're fooling God -- or yourself?

# FAITH AND EFFORT

*Ask, and it will be given to you; seek, and you will find; knock, and it will be opened to you.*

Matthew 7:7

*God created the world out of nothing; so long as we are nothing, he can make something out of us.*

Martin Luther

My mother told me from the time I can first remember that I could be, or do, anything I desired if I just wanted, worked, and tried hard enough. I really don't remember if the work part was included in her guarantee, but I will certainly give my mother the benefit of my doubt. She passed away fourteen years ago, so I can't pick up the phone and ask her.

Was my mother right or wrong?

Scripture tells us we can move a mountain with faith the size of a mustard seed (Matthew 17:20). Jesus told his disciples that anything they asked in His name would be granted to them (John 14:14).

Is Scripture right or wrong?

With all that I was and had, including the lessons taught me by my mother, I figured God had given me all I needed to be able to succeed in any endeavor I "really worked for" as I served Him. In my first two decades of life

I admit that the service aspect of my relationship with the Lord was probably not as high on my daily to-do list as it should have been. However, I never felt removed from God—even during one particular period of complete rebellion on my part when I mistakenly believed God to have categorically failed me.

My genetics provided me with a sturdy, athletic body, enough intelligence to be accepted into membership in Mensa (an organization for folks with an IQ in the top 2 percent of the population), thick red hair, navy blue eyes, and a peaches-and-cream complexion. After making the late childhood move from the shy, frumpy, analytical girl I had been to the slim, chic, and extroverted teen I became, I thought I had the world by the tail on a downhill drag. There was that problematic little complication of my dysfunctional family, but who among us had Ward and June Cleaver as parents?

The list of assets I brought to the game of life seemed to me to be sufficient to provide me with the ability and complete responsibility to establish, direct, and succeed in the life goals I chose. I figured God had already done His share of the work by blessing me with what came naturally. The rest was up to me. I do not mean that I thought I was so wonderful that I had only to announce myself to the world and I would succeed. My belief was more that I had no excuses of extreme poverty, physical handicap, or mental weakness to allow me to cut myself any slack. Anything less than success would be pure failure. You might better understand the pressure I put myself under if I tell you that I got my first A- in sixth grade. I earned all A's up till that time. The A- was such a failure in my parents' estimation that I was grounded until the next report card came out.

Hindsight being what it is, I was actually not as well adjusted as I thought I was, evidenced by those self-destructive moments that occurred in my early adulthood. God never let me go down any of those dark roads so far that I couldn't return to the light. I racked up life lesson after life lesson. A philosophy I still hold today is that we will always make mistakes. They just shouldn't be stupid ones and I count as abject failure making the same mistake a second time. At the moment I can't think of any mistake I repeated, but I guarantee I had no problem finding new and more creative mistakes to make.

Life went on. My life education continued. I learned some very valuable lessons as a result of my marriage to a violent alcoholic. That experience alone could fill many pages, but the details serve no purpose here. Suffice it to say that the Lord set it up so I would make some needed personal changes in order to prepare me for what He had in mind all along. I am forever grateful for this very difficult experience the Lord had engineered. Without it, I would not have learned the Serenity Prayer and, more importantly, learned to live by it. Often the most valuable insights we get are those where the pain of experience is the greatest. There is no greater blessing than a spirit of gratitude, whether we receive it as a gift or learn it the hard way.

**Gratitude**

Indeed, there is a great deal of research and authorship today on the subject of gratitude. Google it and you will find long lists of relevant entries. Gratitude is a wonderful thing. Gratitude engenders generosity. The things that actually matter in life do not reduce as you give them away, they increase. Gratitude, like love and education, is one of these things. Are we born knowing how to be grateful and content? Hardly. Do little children share with others because they come hardwired that way? No, they must be taught to share.

Contentment isn't talked about much anymore. Most people today want to be passionate—passionate about their jobs, passionate about their relationships, passionate about their sports and hobbies. Passion is wonderful, but even a right relationship with God isn't passionate all the time. Anything that burns passionately all the time will burn itself out in no time.

"Too much" is the beginning of discontent. When did "enough" become not enough? Ungrateful hearts breed bitterness and discontent. Practice gratitude. Pray with gratitude. The Lord is worthy and you will feel better.

Decades ago, when the most significant relationship of my life ended I became a typical sinner in rebellion against God. Yet even in that moment of complete dejection I was truly grateful to have been granted the experience that relationship provided. I came to believe that the old saying was true, "It is better to have loved and lost than to never have loved at all."

It took nearly thirty years before I understood why that particular relationship had to end. The reason falls loosely under the category of idolatry. Had that relationship continued, my eyes would have always gone first to his face and not to *His* face. In retrospect, I believe God would have brought me to the same place I am today no matter how that relationship affected me. He would have brought a correction to bear, and it might have needed to be even harsher than I thought it was at the time. God never loses one of his chosen. Ever.

Let's return to what my mother taught me and what Scripture says about what we can do if we just try hard enough or have enough faith. Things went well in my career—not quite in the normal progression, but quite nicely overall. I finished my college degree at night, working one or two jobs during the day. My usual story is that I lucked into management at the age of nineteen, but it is probably more accurate to say that God placed me in a management position at nineteen years of age. So far it seemed my mother's instruction was true; if I worked hard enough I seemed to be able to accomplish whatever goals I set for myself. I wanted to be a self-employed business consultant. All the preparation that was necessary I was able to achieve. For years I worked, I played—but I mostly worked. I was active in my church and blessed with great friends. I pursued my dreams, I ran that 5K race, I bought a motorcycle, and I loved my dog, Snooker.

## Miracles Do Happen

A minor blip in the plan was a small accident that happened a few weeks before my twenty-fifth birthday that ruined my knees. My athletic dreams appeared to have come to an end. I played church softball for a while, but the knees just couldn't cut it. There have been more than a few surgeries over the years and the knee situation alone taught me many lessons, revealing just how merciful and faithful the Lord has been to me. How so? I'll try to make this as concise as possible so we can return to my actual topic. By the time I was thirty-one or thirty-two I woke up each morning and evaluated my walking ability for the day. Would it be a crutch day, a cane day, or a day where no assistance was needed? Such restrictions were slightly irritating at times, but it was not uncommon to see me ride my motorcycle with crutches strapped to the sissy bar with bungee cords.

My knees were horrible in Omaha. After riding a friend's horse for an hour I was absolutely unable to walk. After dismounting (like a rag doll) I depended on the horse to be my crutch until I was able to move again on my own. Doctors in Omaha declared me permanently partially disabled because of my knees. I let that declaration go in one ear and out the other without any intermediate stops in between. My doctors instructed me to sit unless it was absolutely necessary for me to walk or, well, whatever. They had to be kidding. I had way too much drive for that.

The next issue was Menierre's disease that caused me to get so dizzy I would drop to the floor and lay rooted there until the attack passed. In an attempt to find a way to use my excess energy I tried flying small airplanes, but the dizzy thing ruled that option out after just one flying lesson. The next option on my list was to get a horse. Mind you, I had never owned a horse before.

The Saturday after my first (and last) flying lesson I made the decision to buy a horse. By Sunday afternoon my new horse was safely tucked away at a local boarding stable. Even though I had no experience training horses at the time, I bought one that was largely untrained. This was a typical greenhorn mistake, though in my case it seems to have been just part of the plan. How well I remember a lesson my horse taught me about what spurs used in ignorance can lead to when the horse in question is already bucking. I have never repeated that particular mistake. This first horse, and the ones that followed, were my first instructors as I learned to be a horse trainer.

Eventually, my wonderful God-provided husband (of twenty-five years now) and I moved to Phoenix where I became a full-time horse trainer and breeder. I know, I skipped a whole bunch of stuff getting from there to here, but I'm still trying to get back on point.

The year is 1990, and I am now on a ranch north of Phoenix, pursuing my career as a breeder and horse trainer––with ruined knees. Miraculously, however, the Lord blessed me with twenty years of hauling hay bales and feed sacks, starting colts under saddle, training for the show pen as well as for customers who just wanted a safe horse, breeding and foaling out well over a hundred mares, even specializing in training stallions. In 1999, my orthopedic surgeon examined new X-rays of my knees (one more surgery being planned) and said, "You can't do what you tell me you do. It is not possible." Not only possible, but I continued for another nine years after that. My official training career ended twenty years after it began, almost to the day.

**From Miracle to Heartbreak**

So what is the point? Was Mother correct when she told me I could be, or do, anything. In this case, yes. However, the story of my horse career has to include the multitude of heartbreaking experiences my husband and I lived through during our time in Arizona. When we talked about our breeding program, our veterinarians and friends could only say, "If it wasn't for bad luck, you'd have no luck at all."

I will never forget the moment my friend, Jackie, from next door, lay across the hip of a baby colt while I lay over his neck to keep him from struggling up onto a shattered front leg. He had the baby-soft hair that had only known sunlight and air for three weeks. This colt was one you wait your whole life for. Horse people in the area had been calling and coming to see this colt ever since he arrived. Our veterinarian spread the word about him to other clients and breeders. I had already had one once-in-a-lifetime foal; this would have been my second. I guess that when something is truly once-in-a-lifetime there cannot be a second.

Jackie and I lay across the warm little foal, so beautiful and healthy—except for the fracture just below his left knee. The afternoon was fast becoming stormy. We watched the dark clouds gather and roil in the sky as a storm rapidly approached. Though it was barely past midday, the ominous weather brought dark, heavy clouds and howling winds that blew desert sand and manure dust into our eyes. What an eerie, sad picture we must have made as the colt's mother stood over us, expecting us to fix her baby. Jackie, the baby, and I waited for Dr. Rezzonico to arrive.

The colt's registration papers from the Appaloosa Horse Club arrived in the mail the same day he died. His registered name was the same as his famous AQHA daddy's, *Kid Clu.*

My husband stayed in the house. He wasn't able to come out to witness the end of this foal and watch yet another dream die. Over the years we had many wonderful foals that didn't make it. I am grateful to have no regrets about any of them. We did everything right and humanly possible; it was just the luck of the draw, or so it seemed. We wondered if we were being punished, but for what? My walk with the Lord was getting closer and richer by the day. Looking back, I know it was. Just as the darkest night comes just before the dawn, so it often is with God. He was determined to focus my attention more specifically.

Remember, I had been taught that I could accomplish anything if I tried hard enough. I believed God had provided me with all the abilities I needed to take advantage of the opportunities presented. I never prayed for myself. Had I done so, I thought it would seem somehow to be a slap in God's face. It would have been evidence that He hadn't fully prepared me, and how wrong could that be? My prayers were always for others—always. I suppose you can already see where I was going wrong.

John Lyons and his entourage came to our place a couple of times to do his symposiums and private tutoring of students, staying for nearly two weeks each time. One year Gary and Judy Jones of Lamesa, Texas, came to conduct Cowboy Church on a Sunday morning in our covered arena. The Jones parked their camper in front of our house and stayed for a few extra days. What a blessing they were. We opened our hearts to them. Their ministry gave me one of those light bulb moments. What was illuminated in a light so bright even I couldn't fail to see it was -- arrogance.

## Arrogance

My belief in the ability and presumed responsibility for creating every success was actually arrogance. I felt that I shouldn't need God on a daily basis since He had equipped me to take care of myself. Wrong. He was faithful to give me failure after failure—yet without guilt—until I finally fell on my knees to confess that I had reached my limit and could go no further on my own. When I say I went to my knees I mean literally, which for me was no small undertaking. I had no more ability or try to offer. I was spent out. There was nothing left.

The blessing came. God is faithful. He had increased the pressure on me consistently and incrementally until I reached the point where I "gave." This is the same process we use to train horses. God, as the perfect leader, created the plan. He will press us until we *must* move. The pressure disappears instantaneously, miraculously, when we become obedient to Him.

Sometimes a slight pressure may be applied again to reinforce the correctness of our response. By yielding immediately, the pressure—tiny as it may be—disappears again in an instant. If we did not truly learn the lesson the pressure slowly builds again until we must move. Soon, we will elicit the desired response if even a hint of the now familiar pressure returns. The same is true of horses. We begin with soft pressure on a rein to ask the horse to yield its head and neck. Pressure applied slowly, consistently, and incrementally builds until the horse gives to the rein. When the training process is complete, just the motion of our hand lifting results in the immediate, soft yielding of the horse's head and neck. No pressure at all, just a hint, the suggestion, is all it takes.

The process is the same when God works to bring us into obedience. He is always perfect in His timing and precise in His cues, whereas we can never reach that perfection of leadership. Our timing will never be perfect, but, thankfully, horses forgive our minor deficiencies.

**Who Sets the Goals?**

Once the light bulb went on revealing my arrogance, did I find a happy ending? No. I found a beginning. We all have conflicts between the goals we set for ourselves and the plans God has for us. At the beginning of each relationship I have with a horse I have a pretty good idea of what I want the training to accomplish and what my ultimate goal is for that particular horse. The horse will learn in bits and pieces, not understanding where our journey is going to take him. I see the big picture; the horse does not. It is my job to bring the horse through our many lessons and build a relationship that will result in achieving the goal I originally planned.

We only see bits and pieces of the entire plan for our own lives. God alone knows what goal He has established for each of us. In the end, guess whose plan will be accomplished? There is a point at which God bounces people who insist they will not give - who refuse to yield -

from the program. The same is true with horses. I have experienced only a few outright failures in my horse training career that resulted in flunking a horse completely. Part of the original goal may need revision as I learn more about a horse's personality and athletic limitations or discover unexpected talents. Perhaps the horse is not meant to be a rail horse but rather a jumper. The experience of learning and revising goals was mine, not the horse's. I'm not omnipotent or anything like that, but I have enough expertise to evaluate an untrained horse and develop a fairly accurate opinion about what the horse's highest and best use might be. But sometimes I'm wrong and I make the appropriate adjustments as training progresses.

God, however, is omnipotent. He knows beforehand what we can be. Does the fact that I have a pretty good idea of what a horse can become mean that each will attain its highest potential? No. Does God's knowing all we can be mean that each of us will attain our highest potential? Again, no. Every horse brings input to the training process just as we do. Every horse has a degree to which he will yield and continue progressing in their lessons, as do we. Our free will determines how high we climb on our personal ladders of possibility. The degree to which we yield, commit to, and obey our trainer determines how long we remain in the progressive training process and relationship we have with God.

There will be conflict when our plans do not coincide with God's plan. Even after that first light bulb went on I continued to feel pressure. At first it was minor and I was not motivated to make any substantial effort to find a release. God set up changes in our lives that led to our move to Texas. Many things are obvious in hindsight. It is easy to connect the dots of God's handiwork in the rearview mirror. Few, if any, of us get a clear vision looking ahead, while many are given understanding about that which is past

It is a particular blessing to me that many times God revealed the error of my ways to me in hindsight, long after I corrected the problem behavior or wrong position. There was no stigma, no grudge, nothing but greater understanding on my part and a recognition of grace on His. As Baber and I worked through our ten years in Texas the pressure has come and gone with lessons learned and the relationship we have with God deepens. I am getting better at recognizing His gentle application of pressure before He has to make it more obvious to get my attention. Every day I work for greater focus and greater abandonment to His plan and purpose.

My mother was right. I can do anything I work at hard enough—if it fits into God's plan for me. So much energy is wasted on plans that will never be accomplished. Have no doubt, however, that even as we pursue plans doomed to fail, if we keep our eyes and ears focused on our leader, He will be faithful to redirect our feet at the appropriate moment.

Horses learn by making mistakes. Unless I allow them to commit to a mistake, I cannot use the application of gentle correction to let them know they made a wrong choice. As long as the horse's eyes, ears, and body are attentive to me, that horse will never receive anything more than a gentle correction to set its feet back on the correct path. My job is to prepare the horse so the easiest response is the correct one. Only blatant rebellion receives harsher correction. I ask; the horse responds. As the horse's education advances, I must trust him to make good choices.

When a mistake is made, I gently put him back where I intended him to be. God prepares us over time, allowing us to make mistakes which He gently corrects. If we refuse and become stubborn, if we mutiny, His corrections can be harsh. Thank God when they are! Harsh corrections are proof positive that we are still in the program and God is still committed to a successful outcome with us.

When corrections cease it is either because God is letting us soak in our success at that particular level for the purpose of turning our lessons into habit or corrections stop because we have been bounced from the program altogether. When this happens, people may stew around out in the back forty until He calls them home or they are sent to the place all rogue stock eventually goes.

Is it necessary to try and evaluate every desire we may have against God's bigger plan? Not really. Some things we think we want are so obviously off base that we show ourselves to be fools if we pursue them. Would it make any sense for a fairly lame, definitely mature woman to dream of playing in the NFL? If I wanted it enough, if I tried hard enough, could I accomplish that goal? Such a plan deserves to be filed under "stupid." Rather, let us set our goals, walk through the steps necessary to achieve them, and trust God to either reward or correct our actions. As long as we stay focused on Him, all will be well.

What might be possible in your life? With my knees no one would have bet a dollar in 1988 that I would be able to spend twenty years training horses. Yet it happened. People can do things that seem impossible. God gives us talents, abilities, and free will. Your resources will take you only so far if God has other plans, but there is no limit to what you can do when God approves your plans and equips you to succeed.

# COMMUNICATION AND MAKING MISTAKES

*John the Baptist says, "I am not the Christ...He must increase, but I must decrease."*

John 3:30

*Watch for all you are worth until you hear the Bridegroom's voice in the life of another. Never mind what havoc it brings, what upsets, what crumblings of health, rejoice with divine hilarity when once His voice is heard. You may often see Jesus Christ wreck a life before He saves it.*

Oswald Chambers

The peace on earth of the nativity is often misunderstood. "Glory to God in the highest, and on earth peace, goodwill toward men" (Luke 2:14).

The peace and goodwill referred to is not among or between men, but rather that the Christ, the Messiah, has come to *allow* peace between a Holy God and sinful men who believe in Jesus. Earlier in life I thought this verse meant we were to behave peaceably with all mankind and that the goodwill mentioned was between one man and another. I was wrong. Some people still misunderstand the purpose of the Messiah and charge Christians with hypocrisy should they not feel peaceably toward one who behaves badly and sees no reason for repentance. This message of peace and goodwill carries such great magnitude because it assures us we are redeemed and will be able to stand before a holy God without sin, to be without blemish, washed white as snow through the blood sacrifice of Jesus Christ.

However, while goodwill and peace are available at each step in our journey, we are not guaranteed that the road will always be smooth and trouble free. If we are in a relationship with God we are in training, just as our horses are in training. At times the methods necessary to get our attention may cause temporary discomfort or distress. Sometimes we have to watch our friends and loved ones go through times of great trial as the Holy Spirit works through issues with them. We err when we interfere without invitation.

Just as Jesus Christ may often wreck a life before He saves it, likewise the biggest wrecks training horses often occur just before the greatest advancement in communication is achieved.

We must have communication before obedience is possible. As we discovered earlier, the only way to accurately initiate communication with a horse is by the *release* of pressure. The good trainer will allow the horse to commit to a mistake before correcting it. If the horse is always kept just short of making an error, there will never be an opportunity to explain the error. Horses don't speak *human*; humans must learn to speak *horse*. Animal activists and amateurs don't always understand the love and devotion that good trainers apply in the training process. What may appear to an observer as unfair or difficult for the horse is often the most beneficial lesson for the horse as it progresses along the road to obedience and security.

The good trainer provides proper food, water, exercise, mental stimulation, leadership, safety, and security for a horse that will ultimately change its prey animal spirit to a spirit of relationship. Love and affection grow between the trainer and horse as the basics of task and obedience gradually transition to love and devotion. It is the same for human students who over time learn to love their teachers. The most admired and beloved teacher is never the one who gives easy A's. The most loved teacher is the one who instills knowledge, concept, relationship, accountability, and confidence in the student. Think of the teachers you hold in the highest esteem, are they the teachers who instilled in you a desire to achieve or those who gave everyone easy A's? Who taught you to be confident?

If you don't understand how horses learn and relate I ask you to stay out of the relationship between a trainer and horse. Should you limit the good trainer's options to communicate, even when the immediate picture looks bad for the horse, you may handicap the very future of that horse. A very wise man once said, "Don't judge what you don't understand."

I am sure you have heard the old saying, "The path to hell is paved with good intentions." Such clichés and sayings persist because they are based in truth. You may intend to save loved ones from pain or danger by interfering with their relationship with God. But your well-intentioned act may prevent God from doing what He had intended with them rather than helping them. God must be able to have free rein with His children in order to establish communication that builds relationship and, ultimately, obedience.

Jesus never hollers and the Spirit only speaks in a still, small voice. I seldom raise my voice to either a horse or human. If they care, they will listen. If your voice is louder than His, neither you nor your loved one can hear God's Word as intended. In this respect, the Lord is like a horse. The horse escalates its message bit by bit—but not verbally. Good trainers understand what horse body language means and catch what the horse is trying to tell them long before the horse explodes in bucking, kicking, or rearing. These extreme horse behaviors are best understood as screams of frustration or fear. If you do not catch the small communications God sends you, don't be surprised when He begins to increase the pressure to get your attention.

## I Missed the Signs

Have you ever heard of a horse that acted out by exploding with no warning whatsoever? It is doubtful an experienced trainer ever told such a story. It would be the rare case indeed for a horse to escalate into such extreme behavior without giving plenty of advance notice. Most people just don't understand how horses communicate and are surprised when bad things happen. I recently had a conversation with a friend, the father of one of my past students. He was riding his horse, a really nice, well-broke mare. The mare came upon a llama unexpectedly, bolted, and threw him. Although he has recovered from most of his injuries, he now lives with chronic back pain. It is a very unfortunate situation. While he didn't hold the result of the accident against the mare, he sold her and will probably not ride again. As he walked me through the details of the incident it became apparent that it was a tragedy that didn't have to happen. The mare gave plenty of notice that she was in trouble and was looking for leadership. Not finding it, she reverted to a prey animal's primary defensive mechanism: flight.

As we spoke, I asked my friend if his mare had stopped. Yes, she had. I asked if she became stiff, like a statue. Yes, he said, she had. I asked if the mare had lifted her head high into the air as she stared at the llama. Yes, she had. All these are predictable and routine methods of communication for a horse. Abruptly stopping is usually an indicator of a horse sensing danger. The good trainer will evaluate the situation and respond as a leader. Had my friend understood what his mare was trying to tell him while she was still reasonably calm, he could have taken action, defused her escalation of panic, and continued his ride that day and enjoyed future rides.

Well, being a fairly well-adjusted horse, his mare gave my friend another opportunity to provide leadership. The little mare became absolutely rigid, another normal response in the circumstances and another opportunity to change the outcome. She was still willing to be led. Leadership didn't come. The mare's next move was to throw her head up in the air, giving her the best possible view of the alien creature, the llama. Even then there was still a chance to communicate, but the human did not answer. As in most panic situations, communication comes quickly. There wasn't an opportunity for my friend to think about the situation and consider what his best options would be in a leisurely manner. Emergencies call for experience, having the right reaction without having to think about it. Having run out of options, the mare gave up waiting for conversation and bolted. I was sad for both my friend and his nice little mare.

Attentive Christians know God intimately enough to understand that the difficulties they face are usually caused when they miss the signs God provides us. Like horses, God seldom delivers an explosive event in your life without giving warning signals well in advance. Learn to recognize the small signals and signs before your horse, or God, has to explode to get your attention.

Everyone knows someone who lived through a life-and-death moment and seemed to come out of it fundamentally changed. This is one example of God using an explosion to get our attention. Those who learned, who "heard the Bridegroom's voice," are forever changed as a result. Those who wouldn't, or couldn't, hear His voice eventually returned to the place they were before the life-and-death experience occurred and the life lesson, the opportunity to be transformed, was lost.

Without effective communication, lessons can be only minimally successful. Consider the situation today in public schools where students who only understand Spanish are taught in English, where children of the inner-city have a vastly different vocabulary from that of their suburban-raised teachers - the result being ever-increasing drop-out rates.

Communication must be established before education is possible. Education must begin before obedience can be achieved. And obedience is the key to leader-follower relationships.

**Do You Yield from Obedience or Pain?**

Effective training works in one of two ways: (1) results are achieved when the student learns to yield to pain or (2) to yield through obedience.

While some may argue its efficacy, one can indeed learn by yielding to pain, but such techniques produce a stress-induced result. Torture is the ultimate illustration of yielding to pain. The other training method, yielding through obedience, builds a firm foundation upon which future lessons may be built.

Just as torture that exceeds certain critical levels doesn't necessarily produce truth, pain doesn't produce security or confidence—quite the opposite in fact. Learning from the application and submission to pain may produce obedience but will never build relationship.

Students who cram for exams for the sole purpose of getting the best grade possible don't learn much that adds to their foundation. Building a strong base was not their goal from the learning experience because the goal was a grade and not an education. In college I was a master crammer. I would outline the material, study it the night before an exam (even finals), and usually pass with an A. Do you think I retain much of that information today? Nope. This situation illustrates a type of learning similar to that from yielding to pain. The student wants to avoid the negative outcome a poor grade would cause so he works in a manner to get the best grade, not to learn the content of the lesson.

## Cheating

Like human students horses will learn to cheat when they feel no significant relationship with the teacher and they think they can get away with it. When allowed to, horses cheat by doing only what is absolutely necessary to make the pressure go away. No foundation is built. No security, leadership, trust, or confidence is established.

The relationship a student has with his or her teacher is the key. If I had great respect for an instructor I worked hard to gain his or her approval and master the lesson material. In a right relationship, the follower would never dream of cramming information. It would show unacceptable disrespect for his or her teacher.

For several of my teen years I was a figure skater. My pro (instructor) was tough. Really tough. But I highly respected her and worked my tail off to do everything perfectly. The high I felt on those red-letter days when I received a positive comment from her provided ample motivation for me to keep working.

I worked hard, I progressed, and I did quite well. Then my pro retired. I think I was the last non-family student she had. In came the new pro, a really nice younger woman with a great record. She was always so positive and cheerful, even when my work was less than wonderful. People are not driven to excel when "adequate" is perfectly acceptable. I did not respect the new pro because she didn't respect me enough to demand excellence from me.

Likewise, Christians who cheat the process of learning about and from God only harm themselves. If they yield only from fear they will not experience the possibilities the relationship being offered them holds. No foundation is built and they do not receive the immediate benefits of His leadership: trust, security, and confidence. Some horse owners and some trainers confuse cheating with success, errantly giving misplaced affection and rewards to their horse. Research has long proved that what we reward we get more of. If we reward cheating, we are, therefore, training the horse to be a more creative and frequent cheater. If we reward "adequate," then that is what we will get more of. Trust me, both God and good horse trainers know the difference.

**Abuse**

Yes, parents, this also applies to your children. You knew this was beginning to sound way too familiar. Any biologically healthy adult human can become a father or mother, just like any person with access to a horse can call himself a trainer. The truth is it takes well-educated, dedicated, persistent, and obedient parents to properly raise a child. Likewise, it takes well-educated, dedicated, and persistent trainers to properly train a horse. The cause of most disobedient or dangerous teenagers is parents who were absent physically, emotionally, or both.

Worse, some of these kids have abusive parents. Children become vulnerable to abuse when otherwise well-intentioned parents lack the discipline and dedication to properly teach, defend, and love them. Horses suffer abuse when an otherwise well-intentioned trainer is unable to properly teach, defend, and relate to his horse. What was that saying about good intentions and the path to hell?

As leaders, we have the responsibility to teach our children and our horses to communicate, which includes learning to listen. It is our responsibility as parents and horse trainers to build solid relationships. It is far easier to achieve proper relationships with our horses and children if we are rightly related to God. He is the ultimate teacher of right relationships. While it is possible to be what the world would judge a good parent or trainer and not be rightly related to God, it is much more difficult and leaves the child or horse vulnerable.

Without God, there is no ultimate authority and example of how to build relationships. The best plan for success as a parent or horse trainer is to have established our own obedient relationship with God. God's work with us, and ours with Him, teaches us how to communicate and build foundation that allows for even greater understanding in the future. The parent teaches relationship and builds strong foundations that will last for the lifetime of their child. Training a horse is little different. Take advantage of the opportunity you have to learn from the Master trainer.

People who experience a life-and-death issue, who yield only from pain and not obedience, follow the Lord for a time, only to return unchanged to their original errant path. Are their names truly in the Book of Life? We have no way of knowing God's ultimate plan for ourselves, much less anyone else. Just as yielding to pain in horses fails to produce a strong foundation, the same is true in humans who break under pressure but don't make the proper connection with God. Through pain, horses learn fear and hatred, and so do humans. The horse that will not yield except to pain is just as lost as the human who is unwilling to yield to great leadership.

While God is faultless in His communication efforts and training of His children, human parents and horse trainers make mistakes. We have to dedicate ourselves to making constant efforts to succeed in our relationships with our children, each other, and with our horses. All trainers occasionally make wrong judgments. It is important to realize that all error is not sin. My goal in life was to never make the same mistake twice. I keep making new ones because I keep trying. If you are in a right relationship with them, horses are very forgiving creatures. It is my responsibility to listen to the horse as much as it is the horse's to listen to me. Without communication there is no education. Without communication there can be no relationship.

The more we work on our relationship with our Master the more effective leaders we will become in our families, our communities, our nation, and with our horses.

# LEADERSHIP OR DOMINATION

*Woe to those who make unjust laws, to those who issue oppressive decrees.*

Isaiah 10:1

*Wicked men obey from fear; good men from love.*

Aristotle

Effective horse trainers use one of two methods to get the desired response from a horse: obedience (leadership) or domination. All trainers, as they work with ever-increasing numbers of horses, will eventually encounter at least one horse that will not be obedient until it has first been dominated. The good trainer only resorts to dominance when all reasonable attempts at offering leadership have failed. Escalation of action is a natural occurrence in the horse world, part of normal herd behavior. However, once a dominant horse has established its superior position and the inferior horse gives obedience, the overpowering behavior of the dominant horse returns to one of relationship or herdship. The need to prove dominance disappears unless the lower order horse makes a conscious choice to challenge the dominant horse again. It is only human nature that persists in domination after the other has surrendered; it is not the nature of a horse.

There are times when a horse may be dominated by a freak circumstance. As long as the horse isn't injured this can be a fortuitous situation. A friend of mine in Arizona (almost a legend in his ability to turn out an exceptional horse using consistent, quiet methods—he didn't even own a correction bit) shared the story of a rebellious stallion a customer sent to him for training.

The stud was about four years old and just full of himself. He was an idiot to halter, didn't lead willingly, and was just rank. After being in my friend's barn for a few days, the stud was haltered and, as usual, came out of his stall with a bad attitude. This day, however, the stallion slipped on the concrete breezeway aisle as soon as he stepped out of the stall door and fell down. The stud caused the fall himself; my friend had nothing to do with it. Yet, as soon as the horse scrambled to his feet, he had a completely different attitude. Somehow, the stud associated being put down on the ground with the trainer and was prepared to be obedient thereafter.

## A Pretty Problem

A few years ago I had a mare in training that was pushy, nasty, resistant, and barely rideable at a walk when she arrived at my barn. Once I got Lizzie's issues fixed my job was to evaluate her as a possible reining prospect. I was not completely surprised when I discovered that the mare was not at all what her owner said she was. Indeed, this mare was a problem with hooves. She was a pretty problem, which is what got her a home in the first place. But a beautiful face doesn't always come with a beautiful mind.

My customer did not understand the issues this horse came with, not even when the seller told my customer she couldn't buy the horse unless she took her to a trainer. In other words, the mare was dangerous. I messed with the mare on the ground then rode her a bit to check her buttons and figure out where training was needed and where obedience was needed. The initial results were not encouraging. After a couple of rides, I spoke with my customer to ask a few more detailed questions.

I learned that Lizzie was sired by an idiot stallion and out of a mare that was too dangerous to ride so was used instead as a broodmare. Hopefully you will immediately diagnose the problem. If not, let me spell it out. You get what you breed. If you breed an idiot, you will likely get an idiot. It is a truism that the one characteristic you do not want reproduced in a foal is the one you are most certainly going to get. Yes, there are exceptions, but why accept such long odds when there are so many great horses out there already?

With a better understanding of what I had on my hands, I continued working my plan with the inconsistent, unreliable, unruly mare. Lizzie had issues with her ears, so I taught her to be led by an ear. Turning left was a problem, so we learned a left posture and moved every which way possible until she could stay upright and balanced going to the left. Any gait faster than a jog got her tight and pissy. By this I mean she would kick out at my legs and reach around to bite my feet. Just when I thought we had made progress she would find a new way to express herself. This went on for about sixty days. By that time I could do all the basics with her with apparent softness and correct form. But did I trust pretty Lizzie? No.

My customer was suitably impressed with our accomplishments and began to think she had been brilliant in her original assessment of the mare. I tried to tell her otherwise, but I could see she didn't quite buy my opinion. Her horse did really well when she watched me ride her. Indeed, my customer could now ride the mare and do more than she believed possible in such a short time. However, the mare herself was not yet invested in the program. I was teaching her that the proper response always included softness, relaxation, and obedience. She was giving me lip service and was coming along, but I wouldn't have placed a nickel bet on her if push came to shove.

Just as I was about ready to hang it up on Lizzie we had a breakthrough. I was just beginning to trust her enough to actually put one of my good saddles on her. Until I know a horse isn't going to rub me or the saddle into the ground or on a pipe fence it wears a "two-year-old saddle." I set aside a few well-worn saddles to use on young horses that they can roll in, chew on, rub on, and I don't care a whit. This day, however, I put one of my favorite saddles on the mare. Silly me. Lizzie was tied in the grooming rack as she was every day. She had been groomed, vacuumed, and tacked up there at least five days a week for two months. We had worked through the issues of sheets, blankets, ears, and all the rest of her many problems.

For no apparent reason, and usually there is an apparent reason, the mare sat back, broke her lead rope, and went over backwards onto the concrete floor. The grooming areas were covered with rubber mats, but the mare went far enough backwards to get off of them. Was she injured? Nope. Was my saddle? Yup.

What's the point of this story? When that mare stood up she quickly walked over to me and begged me to save her sorry behind. I said, "Well, sure." After that, she was obedient; she put everything she had into her lessons and decided that I was the best thing on earth, even better than her alfalfa. That mare was dominated into obedience and relationship. Like the stallion my friend had, we reaped the benefit of what the horses associated with us even though we really weren't responsible for the circumstances.

I don't know what happened to the stallion my friend had in training, but I can tell you how Lizzie ended up. She was a broke horse after that but didn't transfer her devotion to me to another rider. She would obey, but she wouldn't offer herself up in relationship except to me. The last I heard she was riding fine but would not make a personal commitment to her new trainer or owner. Sometimes it happens that way. I feel bad in situations like that. I make promises to the horse that I end up breaking when I send it home. That is one of the biggest reasons I retired from breeding and training. Even if my body could still stand the work I just don't feel right anymore creating relationships and asking horses to trust me when I know I will not be keeping them. I just can't do it anymore, not even in the short term.

## Bob Gets a Home

When the property that bordered us on the north sold to a new owner the sorrel gelding who lived there, whom we called Bob, needed to be moved. Except for our horses, my husband, and me, no one had even noticed Bob existed for years. The Lord had kept him fed and watered with grass and a tank in the large pasture where he lived. Bob had come to know us a bit and he seemed a decent fellow.

One Sunday afternoon we noticed someone in the pasture trying unsuccessfully to catch Bob. We inquired and were told that the sale of the property was being closed in the morning and Bob had to be removed that day. Of course, the harder you try to catch a horse, the less likely you are to get the job done. Bob was a typical horse, and little progress was being made. As evening neared, I went out and asked if the man standing there with a rope around Bob's neck needed help. He was not able to lead Bob and he needed to get him up to the house and into the waiting trailer. Bob's new owners were there and ready to take him to his new home. We were thrilled Bob was going to have a home, so I went to the barn to get my serious training gear: a rope halter and a long lead rope.

I had never stood next to Bob without a double fence between us. He was taller than I thought and upon closer inspection appeared to be more likely a thoroughbred than the quarter horse I had assumed him to be. After the proper introductory body language, I haltered Bob. The house and awaiting trailer were approximately two hundred feet away. Bob and I "danced" together for a while as I suggested turns to him and let him find his way without putting any tension on the lead rope. We turned right and left; he yielded his hindquarters. I petted Bob and asked for his trust. He gave it in spades. In no time, we arrived at the yard area where I could now see the trailer waiting for Bob. Oh, dear.

Bob's new owners had done the best they could on such short notice to come up with a way to transport him to his new home about five miles away. Once you turned off our road, the farm to market road between where we were and where they needed to go is regularly traveled by semis used in the gas and oil drilling industry traveling at speeds often exceeding sixty miles per hour. There, in front of Bob and me, was a small tractor hitched to a flatbed trailer. The trailer had temporary (and wiggly) sides made from thin sheets of plywood. There was no back, and I assumed the plan was to tie Bob to the front (front what, I had no idea) and drag the trailer home at maybe five miles per hour. As Bob and I stood there assessing the situation, I was in no doubt about at least one thing: I would never violate the trust Bob had placed in me by asking him to get onto that flatbed. No debate, I simply told Bob's new owners exactly that. Bob had exhibited great character and wonderful obedience in a short time. I would not betray him by setting him up to be injured or worse.

After a brief discussion and as the sun was getting ever lower on the horizon, we decided on a plan. My husband went home, hooked up our horse trailer, ramp and all, and drove it over to get Bob. We would take him to his new home. It was the least we could do for Bob. This wasn't my first choice because by taking Bob to his new home I would know where he was going and what his circumstances were going to be. Sometimes we are blessed by not knowing.

The next step in the plan was getting Bob into our trailer. Our trailer is the usual slant load with rear tack compartment, so the horse entry door is about thirty-six inches wide. Not very inviting for a horse that hasn't even had shelter for who knows how many years. Yet Bob learned quickly. When needed, I insisted that he make the appropriate movements using the end of my lead rope on his hip. I trained him to move forward, to turn, and to be obedient. Loading a horse in a trailer to me is actually trailer training. I don't want to just get the horse loaded; I want to build foundation for the next time the horse needs to load and the time after that. The new owners watched and listened attentively as I gave a mini-clinic in the psychology of horses and how one should relate to them. They asked lots of great questions, which showed me they were committed to providing a good and appropriate home for Bob.

As darkness descended, Bob successfully completed his lessons, quietly loaded into the trailer for about the sixth time (I always like to start with six times), and off we went. Bob was unloaded in a gravel parking area across the street from his new home. He led obediently and without any obvious concern to his new grass paddock. Bob was home.

Bob had a family. Bob would be fine. I left my business card with Bob's new family in case they got into trouble. We see Bob every now and then as we drive through the back streets of our tiny town. His owners erected a new roomy shelter within days of his arrival, and Bob is fat, shiny, and loved. My husband and I had regularly prayed for a home for Bob. Our prayers were answered, and we are grateful.

## Balancing Authority and Humility

One of the greatest challenges many horse owners encounter is getting their horse in and out of the horse trailer. Without proper leadership and trust many horses see trailers as either a threat or the exercise of loading as a competition to see who can out-stubborn the other. Owners without the skills to properly train their horse often resort to brutish methods when trailer loading battles frustrate them. Jeremiah (10:21) gave the cause of Israel's calamity as "the shepherds have become senseless (brutish)"; that is, they acted on their own and did not seek God's wisdom and guidance. They did not deal wisely with their fellows. The Israelites devolved into beastly behavior, always seeking to dominate whether necessary or not. Such brutality is not part of God's nature. Trainers who rely primarily on dominating horses do so because they lack sufficient wisdom and are left with a toolbox that contains nothing but brutality.

Other trainers may be efficient but not wise; they have no joy in their work. Indeed, many horse trainers of the 1970s and 1980s didn't even like horses. These trainers grew up in horse families where training horses was the only way they had to pay their mortgages and feed their families. Owning no affection for the horse, these trainer-horse relationships were doomed to ones of dominance and submission. In other cases, trainers may have experienced an early success with one very special horse and tried unsuccessfully for years afterwards to replicate that success. With each failure, the trainer got more and more frustrated. Usually it is the horse that pays the price of a human's frustration.

Even trainers who consider themselves horse whisperers can resort to brutish methods out of ignorance. I witness it on a regular basis and was probably guilty of it somewhere along the line. The trainer thinks he is being relational, acting as a worthy leader—being moral—yet he deceives himself. No human leader or horse trainer has ever lived who did not at some time need someone else to provide perspective or guidance. There is no proper authority without an equal part of humility providing balance. When we are not getting the results we seek we must search out wisdom and direction from a source other than ourselves. To do otherwise is to work using only our limited understanding and keep racking up failures.

*For whoever exalts himself will be humbled and he who humbles himself will be exalted.*

Luke 14:11

Without understanding how to be rightly related to God it is difficult, if not impossible, for the horse trainer to create a right relationship (non-brutish) with a horse. If you are stubborn before the Lord, you will transfer that motivation wrongly to your horse. You stiffen your neck in rebellion and then assume your horse's neck is stiff for the same reason. Could stubbornness be the reason for ole' Sorrel's stiff neck? Possibly, but not probably. It is human nature, not the horse's nature, which believes everyone and everything else works the same way we do. If I am greedy I believe everyone else to be greedy. If I am trusting, I assume everyone else will also be trusting. If I cheat, I will take it for granted that everyone else cheats as well. If I am loving I look for love in others.

## Doing Battle

How can we build our leadership and training skills? What is most important? There is a balance between humility and authority that is necessary to achieve before you are able to understand and replicate right relationship. When rightly balanced we will not resort to dominance unless it is truly what the situation requires. Dominance is only properly used when a horse or human challenges us and there is truly no other way to resolve the matter.

Please understand, choosing dominance is choosing to enter battle. Victory in battle belongs to the one who is dominant when the battle ends. Is battle with a foal ever the appropriate response? As mentioned earlier, sometimes it is necessary to dominate a foal. The weapons of battle with a baby are radically different weapons than those used with a mature horse, but the concepts and strategies are the same. Is it ever appropriate to dominate a human infant? Never.

Dominance is only correct when war is the only option remaining on the table. War must not be unilateral. Initiating a battle is nothing more than brutishness if your opposition does not intend (or has no capacity) to wage war right back at you.

The only exception to a balanced equation of humility and authority is God Himself. There is no higher authority than the Father. Jesus Christ is the perfect example of the proper balance between humility and authority. We would do well to learn from His example. The New Testament is the best textbook for leaders as well as horse trainers. The United States is experiencing a crisis of leadership for this very reason; those in authority seem to have misplaced any humility they may once have owned.

As in Jeremiah's day, our leaders have also become brutish, drawing only from their own understanding. When results (inevitably) fail to meet expectations our government resorts to dominating and restrictive methods to "lead" the people they profess to serve.

I am pleased to clean stalls, as well as do the 101 interesting tasks required of a horse homemaker, most of which are guaranteed to ruin a fresh manicure. How many of our leaders in Washington or our respective state houses would be content to wash the feet of their constituents? Would they even consent to wash each other's feet? Exactly how do they define "public servant"? How many servants have more generous retirement plans than those they serve? How many servants dismiss and criticize those they serve when there is a difference of opinion?

How many servants enact rules that allow them to line their pockets with the hard-earned wages of those they serve? How many servants vote themselves pay increases and benefits? How many servants ride in private luxury while those they serve ride the bus? You get my point, I hope.

The servant has been elevated to royal status. Where is there a more obvious display of arrogance than what we see in our public officials? The root cause of this disastrous reversal of power is the lack of humility in our leaders. Would the military be better served if the privates could pick and choose which commanders got their battle plans enacted?

One cannot wield authority properly without being properly under authority. Good trainers will not be good leaders if they are not properly led themselves. In day-to-day horse training operations an individual who desires to learn the leadership and relational skills of the head trainer aspires to a job as an apprentice. They learn to be correctly authoritative with a horse while under the authority of the head trainer. I understand how to be a good trainer and establish right relationships with my grays by reversing roles and using my relationship to God as the illustration that furthers my understanding. You all know that "absolute power corrupts absolutely." Why? Because absolute authority, by definition, is not balanced by any humility whatsoever.

At the Last Supper, against Peter's protestations, Jesus performed a most humble task and said,

> *If I then, your Lord and Teacher, have washed your feet, you also ought to wash one another's feet. For I have given you an example, that you should do as I have done to you. Most assuredly I say to you, a servant is not greater than his master; nor is he who is sent greater than he who sent him.*

John 13:14-16

As Christ was instructed, so He instructed the disciples. Once you grasp what it means to be absolutely without power or excuse in front of a sovereign and almighty God, you may begin to develop wisdom that will serve both you and your horse well.

# HABIT OR OBEDIENCE

*In everything that (Hezekiah) undertook in the service of God's temple and in obedience to the law and commands, he sought his God and worked wholeheartedly. And so he prospered.*

2 Chronicles 31:21

*Moral excellence comes about as a result of habit. We become just by doing just acts, temperate by doing temperate acts, brave by doing brave acts.*

Aristotle

We took Bo and Copper to a practice match for the Texas Smokin' Guns, a mounted shooting club, part of the Cowboy Mounted Shooting Association (CMSA), an association that governs this unique sport that combines fast riding, period western costume, and shooting balloon targets with single-action .45 caliber revolvers. It's also pretty fun. The CMSA has competition levels suitable for every rider regardless of skill level and value of the horse. Unlike breed association competitions, horses in CMSA events need only be sound and have a name. Okay, they don't really have to have a name, but the announcer has to call them something.

Bo and Copper have been going to shoots every few months or so for the past year so they aren't seasoned shooting horses. Baber and I don't travel long distances just to have fun and we shoot just for fun. Bo has come along really well. My priority has always been to build foundation and confidence. I want Bo and Swizzle to do whatever I ask with confidence and, if necessary, with boldness. So far, Bo and I haven't had any significant setbacks along the way that would interfere with this goal.

Baber and Copper, however, have had a number of bumps along the road. They are both in remedial mode, going back to the beginning and starting to build their confidence again. Relearning is never as clean and precise as avoiding problems the first time, but Baber and Copper are both making good progress. At yesterday's practice, Baber rode Copper for a while with acceptable, though limited, results. I rode Bo.

When we weren't running the pattern ourselves, Bo and I worked balloon duty. Each run uses ten balloons; five each of two different colors. After each rider completes his or her run the balloons have to be replaced so the course is ready for the next competitor. All that is left of each balloon is a tag on a wooden dowel used to hold the balloon in the PVC pole. Bo and I love to pick up these sticks after each run. It lets us practice maneuvering with minimal cues and Bo gets pretty darn used to being on course in a completely relaxed manner.

Bo was really good until his unshod feet got a bit tender on some of the parking lot stones. Once I put protective boots on his front hooves he was happy again. Bo was never owly and it took me a few minutes to recognize that his mild ear pinning and head-tossing meant he was uncomfortable. By putting on his boots I made him now *able* to perform comfortably and he was himself again.

When your horse begins behaving out of character you are the one responsible for figuring out what the problem is and taking whatever action is required to resolve the issue. Physical discomfort is the first possibility you need to investigate. With really obedient and stable horses, you have an even higher degree of responsibility to resolve any minor objections your horse is giving you. Many horses with great temperaments don't create big problems until they are in really severe pain.

Copper did well considering the last couple of times he went into the shooting arena with Baber had been poor or downright disastrous. As a result, Copper now tests his rider for leadership since experience has proved it is not always present. Baber doesn't always pass the test. All trainers make mistakes at times and a rider who isn't a trainer is bound to make even more in such a stressful environment.

After Copper and I picked up sticks for a while, we got to the point where I could guide and rate him mostly with balance and "leg." I decided to test his obedience by riding a stage (riding a full course, shooting the balloon targets at speed). Knowing his history I was only 90-percent sure Copper would perform well without any concerns and with confidence. Knowing there was a 10-percent chance he would get into a bind I had Plan B ready if he started to act out making the event more of a problem than a solution.

Copper was perfect! I passed his test of leadership and he was wonderfully obedient. With this happy result, I pulled his saddle, curried him up, and retired him for the day.

After a really good last stage on Bo we rode out of the arena to the water barrel before going back to the trailer. Bo hasn't quite figured out how to drink efficiently with a bit in his mouth. He sounds like a kid trying to get the last drops out of a plastic cup with a straw; kinda like a splurty vacuum. It was a warm day, and because I had to make sure Bo had the opportunity to drink a sufficient amount of water, I rode him back to the trailer to remove his bridle and put on a halter. While we were still at the water barrel, I had considered dropping the bridle and leading him back to the trailer with just a rein around his neck. It would probably have worked just fine, but we were next to a very busy highway and I wasn't going to chance it.

At the trailer, I dismounted, patted him, hugged his head, took off his bridle, and put on his rope halter. I was just about to loosen his girth when I decided my knees had taken all they could handle for the day.

It was time for a pop quiz to test Bo's level of obedience. The quiz, of course, was really to test my leadership and his obedience. I got back in the saddle with the lead rope in my left hand. Mind you, the rope wasn't even tied around to connect back to the halter forming a continuous loop; it was just a single rope. I had never tried this with Bo outside of our arena, much less away from home.

Off to the water barrel we rode. Bo responded exactly as he would have with a bridle and reins. Shooters were still competing as Bo took a deep, long drink. I sat on him, enjoying our quiet moment together—cherished companionship amid the bustle, traffic, and frequent gunfire.

Perhaps it was time to give Bo a little more difficult quiz. He had certainly aced the pop quiz of riding about with little more than just my legs to direct him. Could I reasonably expect Bo to be obedient if I asked him to go back into the arena and start picking up sticks with no bridle; just a halter and lead rope? So far all my cues of balance and leg were working perfectly. Bo was just as honest and responsive as he had been with a bridle.

If it turned out that Bo wasn't really ready to work and guide in the arena without a bridle, guns blazing, and horses racing around at breakneck speeds -- I did trust him to be reasonable if I had to change plans quickly. After giving due consideration to the matter, I determined we would not be jeopardizing our safety or that of the others in the arena by leaving the bridle behind.

Into the arena we went, barely squeezing through the chute that was mostly blocked by three riders watching the competition and chatting among themselves. I had already tested "whoa" without using any hand or rein cues at all and was confident that whatever other issues might arise, Bo would stop whenever I asked.

I sent Bo down the line of cones and poles picking up sticks at a rapid trot, turning easily as we negotiated the course. Perfect! Back we loped to the balloon staging area to turn in the sticks. We side-passed up to the bucket, dropped our sticks over the fence and returned to the rail at the end of the arena to wait for the next shooter to finish the course. So far no one even noticed Bo wasn't wearing a bridle, not even my husband. I love this horse!

After the next shooter screamed back across the finish line toward us, Bo and I headed out again to pick up the sticks from spent balloons, taking a different path through the cones than we did the last time. We were briskly heading to the farthest cone, the one nearest the spot where Bo and I had spent most of our day waiting during runs.

Habit of task kicked in. I tried to steer Bo in the direction away from our usual resting place where he thought we were heading. He didn't turn away from my instruction—he just didn't turn at all. Instead of making a 90 degree turn to the right as my balance and leg requested, Bo just went straight until we arrived at the arena fence, about thirty feet ahead. Not far to the left was our usual spot. Bo had been returning to that place all day long. I knew he thought we should be going there, which required a left turn. But my request had been to turn right. Yet I had no right rein. Using the fence to my advantage, I pushed the lead rope up his neck a bit (usually I neck rein at the shoulder) to communicate a boundary and exaggerated my left leg position. I simply held those cues until Bo figured it out. Habit of task had created the confusion; habit of obedience would resolve it.

## Quit While You're Ahead

Off we loped again in good order. A glimmer of doubt began dawning in my mind. The concept of actually having options other than obedience could occur to Bo after this exercise, so I did what any good leader would do in the circumstances. We quit on a high note. I rode Bo back to the trailer. Bo finished the quiz with 100-percent correct responses. I dismounted, pulled his saddle, and gave him a good rub down and a carrot.

What did I learn? First, I had remembered to check my motivation before beginning the exercise. Was I just trying to show off? Maybe just a little. I'm only human. Bo was a star. Copper also passed his own test of obedience with flying colors. We still have work to do, higher levels to achieve, but this was a very good day.

# THE 153 FISH PRINCIPLE

*The disciples "got into the boat, and that night they caught nothing."*

*And He said to them, "Cast the net on the right side of the boat, and you will find some." So they cast, and now they were not able to draw it in because of the multitude of fish.*

*Jesus said to them, "Bring some of the fish which you have just caught." Simon Peter went up and dragged the net to land, full of large fish, one hundred and fifty-three; and although there were so many, the net was not broken.*

John 21:3, 6, 10, 11

Whenever I have a significant lesson with Bo or Swizzle, the Lord takes the opportunity to give me a corresponding lesson as well. Whenever my personal ego balloon starts getting a little over inflated I can always count on the Lord (or a horse) to let a whole lot of the air out. And that's a good thing, 'cause too much air can cause a balloon to burst. This morning the Lord showed me how the test of obedience applied to me. God is so amazing. Each time this "coincidence" of parallel training occurs, I am less and less surprised. I am, however, increasingly grateful that God loves me enough to continue my training day after day.

Much has been written about the mystery of the 153 fish caught by the disciples in the twenty-first chapter of John. Because the result of Jesus' directions were so precisely related in the text—"153 fish" and "the net did not break"—biblical scholars surmise that there must be a great message to Christians hidden in the specifics of these gospel verses. Most of the writing on the story of the 153 fish has to do with the number itself: 153.

If you search the Internet for commentary on these verses, you will find a host of machinations, algebraic formulae, and intricate calculations of how the number 153 may be significant. The simplest explanation was that the number 153 represented the total number of fish species in the sea, perhaps a metaphor for all the peoples on earth. Well, that theory has since been proven to be false.

Other equations deal with the number of days Jesus lived on earth: 12,240. How is this significant? If you multiply 153 by 80, you get 12,240. One reads in various other places that Jesus' ministry on earth lasted 918 days, or 153 multiplied by 6. There are many sources who believe the number 153 to be significant as it relates to the number of generations from Adam to Christ and beyond, 77 plus 76. This equation always includes a footnote, as the numbers don't quite work out without some qualification.

May I suggest another explanation of the story of the 153 fish? As a very simple soul myself, the various and creative ways others use to prove the number 153 to be of particular significance are interesting but not particularly meaningful to me. How do such mathematical exercises assist us in our daily walk with Jesus Christ? The story of the 153 fish begins, "In this way Jesus showed Himself " (NKJV) to the disciples in a third and final time before returning to sit at God's right hand.

*In this way*, what I call the "153 Fish Principle" is the application of the gospel's message in one short story. Jesus gave the disciples and, indeed, all Christians, one final, perfect illustration of how we are to live in right relationship to Him. In these verses we find seven of the disciples fishing—men who were specifically called and chosen to build the church of Christ and who shared all of Christ's ministry with Him. Day after day these men walked with the Lord. They had already been selected to receive the Holy Spirit and carry on the ministry of Jesus Christ.

Remember, these men were experienced fishermen. They weren't weekend anglers. The seven disciples set out that night on the sea to fish by their own choice, doing what they well knew how to do. The Holy Spirit had not yet sent them out on their ultimate missions. These disciples, these expert fishermen, spent all of that dark, barren night working, working, working, letting down their net again and again only to haul it back in empty. Imagine the frustration they felt doing what they knew how to do yet experiencing complete and exhausting failure.

One final time Jesus instructed His disciples. He told them what to do: "Cast your net." He told them where to cast it, "on the right side of the boat"; and He told them when to act—to act now. The disciple's expertise at fishing yielded nothing. The fact that they had physically walked with Jesus Christ did not produce success. The key to their success that morning on the sea was obedience to His direction, resulting in the incredible, abundant fruit of 153 large fish.

Obedience to Jesus Christ produced the miraculous catch, not the election of the disciples and not their specific knowledge of fishing. What was Jesus telling these men this one last time before sending them off on their own ministries and for most to their martyrdom? Jesus was showing them (and us) that a right relationship with Him produces obedience—and only by acting in obedience can we achieve success.

Not long before I realized I was writing this book I returned to a business consulting practice that had been mostly dormant during my years in the horse industry. I had spent six months in near retirement when the Lord gave me a new assignment. He was specific and thorough, and I was both surprised and pleased to discover I was still capable and relevant. It was clear that I was now working for God, at His direction and at His pace. He cleared the road when needed and opened doors in front of me. I basked in the luxury of working His plan at His direction. As time progressed, however, I started trying to sit in the manager's chair, beginning to review marketing and promotion options to build my practice. I knew how to do it; I had done it all before.

I began to worry (well, I didn't worry, but considered) what my next moves should be for my consulting practice—until the answer came. It was not a new message but confirmation of what I already knew. Confirmation came by way of the experience I had with Bo at the Texas Smokin' Guns practice where he defaulted to the habit of task until my gentle correction brought him back into obedience. The message was not to fall into the habit of task, doing what I knew how to do. I was gently but firmly "informed" that I was to remain obedient and wait for instruction from the Boss.

My work is no longer mine to direct. I am in a new phase of my relationship with the Lord. The habit of task must be replaced with the habit of obedience. It is not a quick work and I know there will still be quizzes or tests that I will not ace. In the meantime, Bo and Swizzle are wonderful gifts for the relationship I enjoy with them, and they serve me well as illustrations of the lessons meant specifically for me.

This story of Jesus and His disciple fishermen is absolutely on point for the lesson I learned today and hope to remember tomorrow when temptation to revert to task arises again. Peter and the disciples fished all through the long night without success. They caught absolutely nothing.

The first time Jesus (the Spirit) told me to cast my net, I came up with an assignment I wouldn't have thought possible for a first project back in the consulting saddle, years away and far removed geographically from my prior work. I was given a huge project and allowed to complete it well.

The next specific work I was given was this book, *Amazing Grays, Amazing Grace.* I expected to return to consulting and speaking. It never occurred to me that I would be writing again, especially on a non-business subject.

The "153 Fish Principle" is simple: do *what* Jesus instructs, *where* He instructs, and *when* He instructs. Rest all on Him, not on your own abilities and talents. Apart from Jesus Christ, there is only exhausting failure. Leave behind the long, dark, cold, unproductive nights of self-direction. Obedience will yield success.

My conclusion? I will continue to cast my net where He tells me and when He tells me. That's my job. I am confident that in His time I will receive instruction for each new catch as He directs. My obedience is the heart of it. In return, I am blessed by my relationship with Him.

# TEST OF LEADERSHIP

*Not that I have already attained, or am already perfected; but I press on, that I may lay hold of that for which Jesus Christ has also laid hold of me.*

Philippians 3:12

*How we spend our days is, of course, how we spend our lives.*

Annie Dillard

When comparing the habit of task and the habit of obedience we discover two major differences: one builds foundation for future learning, the other does not; and one builds relationship, and one does not. Someone once said that bad habits are like a soft chair—easy to get in to but hard to get out of.

One early spring weekend we went to Cleburne, Texas, for another practice shoot. Having never been to this arena, Copper and I went out first to warm up. I try to be sure that he and Baber aren't going to get into trouble. As the trainer for them both, I am responsible for their safety and assuring that they build confidence and not patterns of inconsistency.

This was the day Copper taught me about tests of leadership from a horse's perspective. Baber and Copper had experienced some pretty serious wrecks when they began competing in mounted shooting events. When we first took up mounted shooting, Copper was more confident than Bo, and it seemed that Copper and Baber would be the shooting stars of the family.

However, the foundation they had to work with was not strong enough, and Baber is not an experienced horse trainer. Events stacked up against them and compounded until the crisis Copper found in Baber's leadership resulted in mutually bad experiences.

Bo and I have been slowly and steadily building our confidence without any setbacks or difficult places. I am careful to never ask more than Bo is ready to give, and I am a fanatic for getting "correct" before asking for "fast." As an experienced horse leader I know how to proceed in an orderly fashion even if it looks to others like we spent a year in kindergarten. Well, in a way, we did. Bo was barely broke when we started going to shooting matches. Sometimes choosing to take things slowly can be the fastest route to ultimate success. The result of my method was to build a relationship that allowed Bo to go from kindergarten to middle school in only a few months then to completely skip high school and begin working on college-level lessons.

As a result of the bad experiences Copper had, he needed to go back and pick up remedial classes in order to work through the issues those smash ups created. While I had not been personally involved in the wrecks, ultimately they were my responsibility. I had not supervised Copper's education with Baber closely enough. It was my failure that left both Baber and Copper with more confidence in having a bad outcome than in having a good one. At least I know how to fix the mess I made. It only took those one or two events to seriously damage Copper and Baber's relationship—at least at shooting matches.

The good news is they are doing better, but it is now imperative that I structure every ride to build Copper's obedience and confidence in our leadership.

Having a wonderful nature, Copper taught me a lesson about leadership in Cleburne that day. I rode him around the unfamiliar arena, looking for any places where he might tighten up or exhibit fear. I was working on creating the habit of task in this new environment and the habit of obedience in our relationship. My message to the horses I train is that they may be confident I will never ask them to do anything that will hurt them; they may freely obey without fear. Since Copper knew that my leadership record with him was less than perfect, he decided to put it to the test. What a smart horse.

Copper worked very nicely in the arena, loose and relaxed. He accepted pressure, giving every correct response. As I warmed him up, I considered limiting our tasks to only walking, trotting, turning, and stopping properly and lightly. My logic was to not introduce the lope as part of today's habit so Copper wouldn't interpret a miscue from Baber as a request for a lope.

Baber is uncertain when riding Copper faster than at a trot. Part of Copper's remedial training is the creation of new physical habits and physical frame at the lope. We need to create new muscle memory. Copper has particular issues with his left lead and needs to practice, practice, and practice until the correct form is his default form.

**The Test**

Sometimes this plan of not doing a particular exercise is a good one; sometimes it is not. With horses, there is no one right, absolute answer to any question. In circumstances like this, it is important that I analyze my motivation before making a decision. Am I really making the situation safer—or am I avoiding one of those troublesome doors we avoid in fear of what lies behind it? Was I afraid Copper would be disobedient if I asked him to lope and I would have to commit to a training session on the spot? I decided to skip the lope and rode him back to the trailer so Baber could get on and ride.

Copper and I left the arena through a different gate from the one we had entered. Tucked in behind a rail fence and paneled gates was a set of wheels attached to loose axles. Each axle had just one old wheel on one end, the other end resting in the dirt. They reminded me of the tinker toys I played with as a child. Fences formed a twenty-foot wide alleyway from the gate exiting the arena to another about sixty feet away. The alley fences formed one side of pipe pens built on either side of the alley. Copper saw those wheels hiding behind the fence, sucked his body backwards like the tide going out, and gave me every hint he was prepared to flee. I firmly, but gently, kept Copper facing those fearsome monster wheels, letting him stare at the wheels for about five seconds. I knew those wheels weren't going to move or make any sound, so there was absolutely no valid reason for Copper to be concerned about those hunks of iron. His behavior surprised me, as Copper is not usually a spooky horse. Go figure.

I asked Copper to take one step toward the wheels, and then I instructed him to stop. If you are in a situation similar to this, don't wait for your horse to decide to stop, tell him where to stop. As we already know, he who controls the feet wins. Always keep your horse in a place of obedience.

If you begin to sense that your horse is about to refuse to go forward, ask him to back up. Then ask for one or two steps forward. Stop. Relax. Pretend you haven't a care in the world. Continue forward a step or two at a time.

Stop. Relax. Remember, your horse must be moving when you say whoa. If this doesn't seem to work or if your horse just sulls up and won't go forward, steer into a different angle and try again.

Copper and I stepped forward. We stopped. After another second or two, I asked Copper to walk by the wheels. In the alley there was a limited area to work with, and Copper put as much distance between himself and those wheels as the fence allowed. I did not allow him to cheat his form; I maintained correct movement and position, requiring Copper to go where I asked. I walked him by the wheels a few more times until he looked at them and became soft and obedient again.

We left the arena. Baber got on Copper, and I got on Bo for the first time that day. I warned Baber about Copper's reaction to the wheels and gave him instructions on what to do if Copper began to react badly to the wheels as he and Baber prepared to walk through the alley. Not surprisingly, when Copper and Baber rode by the wheels, Copper didn't appear to remember that they existed much less that he acted as though they might eat him only five minutes earlier. Copper was so cool that butter wouldn't have melted.

The Lord showed me that the wheel exercise had been a test of my leadership. Horses are pretty smart if we simply take the time to understand them. Copper wasn't going to wait until something came up that would really concern him before finding out if my leadership was up to his requirements. Copper wanted to know right at the get-go if he could trust me.

We read in the Bible that if we cannot be trusted with small things, how then can we be trusted with important things? As Jesus said in John 3:12, "If I have told you earthly things and you do not believe, how will you believe if I tell you heavenly things?"

This is exactly the test Copper gave me. He wanted to know if he could believe me in a simple matter, the wheels. If I failed that small test, there was no way he was going to follow my lead in any serious matter, like shooting guns.

After Copper and Baber had hung out in the arena for about an hour, I noticed that Copper was responding less and less precisely to what Baber was asking him to do. Baber was becoming less confident, and so was Copper. It was time for Copper and I to work through another lesson together. Baber tied Bo up back at the trailer for me, and I got back onto Copper.

Heading out to the arena again with Copper I decided to up the ante. It was time to lope. I asked Copper to pick up a nice, easy lope. He gave me a half-hearted crow hop before taking the lead I'd requested. Wrong response. I pulled him around quickly, and while he was curled like a cat, I used my spur to send his hip in a circle around his front end. Once he gave completely to the pressure, I lined him out straight again and without any hesitation asked for the lope again.

This time Copper was just as sweet and light as he could be. We toured around at an easy lope for a few moments and then I asked him to pick up his left lead, the one that is more difficult for him. Copper was obedient, and I patted his rump and scratched his neck as we loped around the pen. I decided to run a full shooting pattern on him, gunfire and all. The habit of obedience won the day. Copper did precisely as I asked and was a completely happy camper from the time we crossed the timer line at the beginning of the run to crossing again at the end.

Copper tried me, I passed his test, and his confidence in my direction grew. What a glorious day.

## Another Amazing Gray

As we build a habit of obedience, do we try to teach our horses to always ask for permission before reacting to a stimulus? Absolutely not. I want the benefit that the horse's superior vision and hearing bring to our relationship. Good trainers want to preserve their horse's freedom and personality. When a horse spooks or refuses to obey, we have but a split second to determine if there is a valid reason for the horse's negative response. The situation must then be handled appropriately.

Years ago I was training a gray quarter horse gelding for a customer. My customer liked the horse, but she was frustrated when he would quit loping and that he stopped on his front end rather than from behind, as is correct and most comfortable. My job was to tune-up the gelding so he could be sold.

This gelding was a stout, good-looking fellow and sure seemed to be kind. My habit at that time was to do each horse's daily lesson in the arena and then ride out into the desert to cool off and check how well the horse handled trail riding. This routine allowed me to find any hidden issues with traffic, birds, animals, terrain, or other unexpected situations. When I represented a horse, I always wanted to know as much as possible so I could either fix any problem that came up, or at least accurately relate strengths and weaknesses to prospective buyers.

One day this good gray gelding and I were out in the desert after a successful lesson when he abruptly stopped. No prancing, no nervousness, and no apparent reason for coming to a dead stop. I asked him to move forward. He very politely refused. *What in the world is wrong with this horse?* I was puzzled. I asked him to move forward again. Again, he politely refused and continued to calmly stand rooted to that spot.

Then I saw it: a rattlesnake coiled under a creosote bush about five feet in front of us. What a great horse. He refused to obey my request to move forward because he had more information about our situation than I did. That good gray gelding had been perfectly polite in his refusal. My policy is to always give the benefit of my doubt to the horse. Although my requests for him to move forward were firm, they never escalated past "firm." That marvelous gray did not escalate his refusal from that of being absolutely polite—so I did not escalate my requests either. If this gelding had been taught to always yield to his rider without question, we could have found ourselves in a very bad situation. That gray took care of me. I was grateful. I acknowledged the snake, petted the gelding's neck, and guided him in a wide berth around the rattler.

Just to finish the story about this good gray gelding, I schooled his lope and stop, so all was well. It really wasn't that difficult a task. I called my customer to come ride him and check my work. She was a good-sized lady without great hands or seat—in other words, she wasn't a well-schooled rider. As she rode that good gelding, his issues began to surface again. She asked him to lope. He was immediately obedient. He didn't lope for long, however, before he simply stopped. She tried again, so did he. Again, he stopped. Before she got on that good gray, I had demonstrated for her how well he performed. He loped beautifully and stopped on a dime. Not one time had he quit while I was riding him. Before giving my customer the chance to get frustrated, I explained to her why that good gray gelding was quitting with her.

My customer was not exactly petite, and as I mentioned earlier, not a well-schooled rider. As that good gray began to lope with her, she began to lose her balance. Each successive stride put her closer to the point where she could have bounced out of the saddle completely. As soon as her situation became precarious, that good gray gelding would stop and quietly stand, allowing his rider to regroup and get back in the middle of the saddle. That wonderful gray gelding was simply taking care of her as he had with me out in the desert. What a guy. If I could have, I would have bought him on the spot. Even though he had to be uncomfortable with his rider's lack of skill, he just did whatever she asked until his greater experience and kindly concern for his owner prevailed and he stopped.

Great credit goes to my customer for understanding and appreciating the reality of the situation. She didn't just have a decent horse with a couple of issues; she had a great horse that could be counted on to take care of her in any situation. My customer had her very own amazing gray. I am pleased to report that the good gray gelding was no longer for sale at any price. My customer decided that riding lessons would be a good idea, bless her heart. I loved my customers, and I love happy endings.

As a trainer I want obedience and patience from my horses. I also want them to be confident and free to instruct me when necessary. Worthwhile relationships are not one-sided. No one can be a great leader if there is no one willing to follow. God requires obedience and commitment from us. Yet He leaves us free to exhibit the unique personalities He gave each of us. Unlike me, He knows where all the snakes are, but the essence of the lesson is the same.

Do you have the habit of task or of obedience? Do you yield from pain or through obedience? Are you wonderfully confident in your relationship with Jesus Christ? As you blissfully proceed along life's path, have you ever found yourself stopped short without any obvious explanation? Perhaps there is a snake coiled and hiding just in front of you. Be very careful before pushing ahead. Some obstacles are there in order that we may learn to overcome them, and some are deliberately put before us in order to redirect our feet.

Copper taught me how to be both a better leader and a better follower. That good gray gelding taught me that things are not always what they first appear to be, and sometimes the best plan is to listen rather than to direct.

# OBEDIENCE AND BONDING

*And this is love: that we walk in obedience to his commands.*

2 John 6 (NIV)

*Obedience without faith is possible, but not faith without obedience.*

Unknown

Relationship building is a progressive exercise. Attractions to others may be instantaneous; but strong, meaningful relationships are made in an orderly, predictable manner. Even the relationship between a mother and her child follows an established path of development. The initial attraction is physical, and hormonal, as she feels the baby move inside her during the pregnancy. At birth, strong hormones create a powerful attraction and the bonding process continues.

Many research studies have proven the link between hormones and physical touch with the strength of the resulting emotional cord that continues to connect mother and child throughout their lifetimes. Fathers are bound to their children first by the relationship they share with the mother. A separate relationship begins along its own structured and predictable way when the father starts physically caring for the child and by making a commitment of time, energy, and proximity to his offspring. Proximity is of utmost importance. Absent fathers and mothers do not have elementally strong relationships with their children.

Anyone who has raised a child can testify to the need for a strong bond with his or her infant child. Were it not for that great love, that relationship, all two-year-old children would be shipped off to military preschool just to get them out of the house. Hormones initiate protective feelings; relationships support and continue them. Without relationships, the stress of caring for children could easily exceed the perceived benefit. We do it for love.

From the child's perspective, relationships with the mother begin by simple need. Nourishment, warmth, and the need for protection are given by the mother and father. There is no universe to an infant save the humans who care for her. As the child grows and matures, her world enlarges. This expansion results in more variety of experience and opportunity for relationships with others besides the parents. Siblings become recognizable as separate humans. The child begins to become aware of, then process, her environment. Soon she is aware of other people outside the family. Preferences begin to emerge as the child's personality forms and is expressed.

At this very early stage, the habit of obedience, or lack thereof, begins. It is never too early to provide a child with structure and boundaries as they begin to learn more about loving relationships. Indeed, structure and boundaries are a vital part of strong, meaningful relationships. Structure, boundaries, and consistency are the pillars that support security, trust, and confidence.

## Mares, Foals, and Me

In horses, the mare-foal relationship is very similar to that of the human mother and child. The degree to which a mare understands who is causing that movement in her belly during pregnancy is unknown, but God has certainly handled the matter through the use of hormones. From conception through birth, hormones are busy, making the mare at least physically aware that she is pregnant and also providing the massive amount of hormone that causes her to pass the afterbirth, bond with her foal, and produce milk to nourish it. Just as with human mothers, most mares will claim their foals very soon after birth and defend them to the death from all threats and predators.

When does the relationship building process between a human and a foal begin? It starts as soon as the foal is aware that a human is there. I have had the privilege of being present at more than a hundred foal births. I have caught more than one foal in the process of entering the world midway between the standing mare's body and the ground, trying to keep the umbilical cord intact long enough to complete the passive transfer of blood from the mare to the baby. How effective and helpful I am to the foaling process depends entirely on the strength and quality of my relationship with the pregnant mare.

One maiden mare (having her first foal) and I enjoyed a particularly close relationship. When stage three labor began, she had no idea what was happening. She whinnied and nickered for me to come and hold her hoof. She wanted me to be right there with her to provide security and support. What a privilege. Together we welcomed a wet, warm little chestnut filly into the world. As on many other occasions, this foal and I began our relationship while her hind feet were still inside the mare. Too soon? Certainly not in this case.

There are as many opinions about how and when the human-foal bonding process should begin as there are opinions about how human babies should be birthed. My opinion is that only well-informed, experienced, emotionally invested people should make such decisions. If you don't truly understand and love mothers, babies, and the entire birth process, well, you may not have a helpful opinion. Book learning is fine, but some things require hands on, down-in-the-wet-straw experience.

For years I attended the birth of every new foal. The expected foals were all valuable in an economic way in addition to their intrinsic worth as individuals. In the vast majority of instances a mare has no need of assistance and really doesn't want human interference. However, any complication during the foaling process is nearly always a matter of life and death. With experienced mothers, if I planned on not attending the birth physically, I at least checked to make sure that labor proceeded normally, without complication.

The many, many nights I spent sitting in front of a closed-circuit TV screen watching mares prepare to foal allowed me to begin making informed choices about when and under what circumstances I would actually be physically present at each birth. I discovered that for most mares, my presence in the stall, or at the stall door, caused them to lie down only to get up again and again during labor. When left alone, many mares lay down in the spot they eventually give birth without all the jostling around. Getting up and down is especially dangerous once the foal's front feet and head are already delivered.

Over time I developed the opinion that well-adjusted mares should have plenty of time alone with their new foals to allow the bonding process to proceed without human interruption. After the first twenty-four hours, I began the process of building a relationship with the new baby. Structure, boundaries, and consistency are introduced, even at this very early stage of the foal's life.

Of course, the structure and boundaries were those of body language, space issues, and quickly resolving any contest of wills. I used the method of communication the foal was preprogrammed to understand. The foundation we lay in the first day or two of that foal's life will remain in place as long as we have a relationship with it. Most good trainers today will understand the techniques I use to construct the foundation I will build upon throughout the foal's life.

Can even a very young foal exhibit wrong behavior? Absolutely. There will eventually come a day when every spoiled or recalcitrant little brat will need to learn obedience. Those of us who love horses know that they need structure, safety, consistency, relationships (the herd), and accountability just as people do. It is tragic when horse owners are ignorant of the facts. It is even more tragic when human parents ignore, or are ignorant of, the needs of their children.

There will always be a hard lesson in the future for a foal that wasn't taught structure and boundaries. They will be insecure and may even be dangerous.

There will always be a hard lesson in the future for human children who are not taught to respect boundaries and recognize when obedience is required. They are also more likely to be insecure, unhappy for sure, and potentially dangerous, if only to themselves. Children with self-destructive tendencies will eventually become self-destructive adults if their paths are not changed.

Obedience is a habit. The habit of obedience is acquired over time with frequent, regular repetition of consistent experience until obedience is an automatic response. Practice, practice, practice.

Our relationship with God is built in the same way as the relationship of mother and child, or mare and foal. It develops over time, requires structure and boundaries, consistency and proximity. Structure and boundaries are given to Christians in the Bible and through the work of the Holy Spirit. The first lesson we are to learn is that of obedience. If we do not, there will always be correction and consequences. Once the habit of obedience is established, other lessons may be learned.

The child begins to learn words, reading, numbers, and how they are to interact with others outside the family. The horse moves from simple obedience to more complex skills and maneuvers. The Christian moves to a deeper level of spiritual communion with the Lord and learning how they are to properly lead their lives to glorify God. In every case, whether child, horse, or Christian, the habit of obedience must be regularly tested and maintained. Relationship can only grow with a commitment of time, consideration, and proximity. Parents and horse trainers are responsible to be properly prepared before lessons begin. God is never unprepared.

**Relationship Triangles**

The habit of obedience must be firmly in place before adding complications to the relationship of parent and child, trainer and horse, God and man.

Let's consider how adding another individual to the mix changes relationships. Bo is learning to be a pony horse. That means that I ride Bo and lead another horse alongside. My requirement for Bo is to willingly and softly go where I ask him at whatever speed I ask. He is to perform as if the second horse is not even there. The horse being ponied is expected to stay on my right side (we will add the left side later) with its head at my knee. The test is for me to be able to comfortably drop my right hand down and find the head of the horse being ponied in the perfect position to be petted or scratched on the forehead. I should not need to rely on my reins to guide Bo, and the one being led should be in the correct position without any tension on the lead rope. The ponied horse is responsible to stay where it belongs without having to be reminded.

Bo is well on his way to being a great pony horse. He has already proven that he can take a hard hit and remain steady should a horse being ponied resist and sit back with its full weight on the rope dallied to my saddle horn. Bo is to walk, trot, or lope as requested, no matter what the other horse does. And, when asked, he has been obedient to move into the other horse, pushing its hip around when needed.

Once I moved Bo from task-oriented work to relational work, the whole dynamic changed. Bo and Swizzle are part of a herd. They live out in pasture with Asti and Copper most of the time. In the herd pecking order, Bo is higher than Swizzle. It is an almost daily occurrence for Bo to push Swizzle around by putting pressure on her at her hip and driving her where he wants. This is Bo's reality of his relationship with Swizzle. They like each other and seek out each other's company, but when push comes to shove, Bo is the boss over Swizzle.

Bo and I have a well-established relationship. He obeys me. Where ponying is concerned, Bo has displayed a habit of obedience appropriate for his level of training. So has Swizzle. She has learned how to be obedient as the ponied horse. Whether at a walk or trot, she keeps her forehead right at my hand or knee as if she wasn't even haltered. Swizzle is confident in this arrangement; life makes sense to her. Bo, on the other hand, is now a little confused. Actually, I wonder if he thinks I am confused.

When he ponies Copper, Bo is as steady as a rock. He stays right where I want, straight as an arrow, guides and responds just as if we weren't leading Copper with us.

But Bo isn't the same when we pony Swizzle. He isn't exactly disobedient, but he tries to drift just a bit to the left, away from Swizzle, rather than tracking straight and easy. He keeps running into my left leg, and I have to repeatedly cue him to get back straight. He keeps a concerned right ear focused on Swizzle even though she is just blissfully popping alongside without a care in the world. What is the difference? Why am I getting a different reaction from Bo? He is 100 percent obedient and solid when ponying Copper, his good buddy, but isn't sure he's completely with the program when ponying his little friend Swizzle. The difference is one of relationship. Bo needs to learn to obey even when he doesn't understand why he is being asked to do something that to him seems wrong.

Why would Bo think it wrong? Bo's habit of obedience to my direction when we pony has been complicated by his relationship with Swizzle. This third wheel in our relationship equation isn't tracking correctly from his perspective. Bo currently believes that the power position is off the hip of the other horse. When he moves Swizzle around the pasture, he is on her hip, gently pushing and driving her along. He is the top banana. As a pony horse, he leads and the horse being ponied is on his hip, just as if it were driving or pushing him along. When we pony Swizzle, Bo thinks that his position relative to Swizzle is backwards and that she now holds the position of power. This reversal of status, in his mind anyway, taxes his commitment to obedience. He is actually doing pretty well, considering, but we have work to do. Bo must learn to obey no matter how bizarre the circumstances seem to him.

What I learned from Bo and Swizzle is to learn to obey the Lord even when I don't understand the "why." It's hard to be obedient, especially when our pride is involved. I marvel at just how obedient Bo is. Imagine you are forty years old with twenty years of experience as a registered nurse. You have been told that you are to serve in a subordinate position to an eighteen-year-old in the annual flu-shot program at your church. Not only is the kid not a health professional but you know this kid and he's lucky to get his shoes on the right foot each morning. How could you softly, happily, and obediently await his instruction. This is pretty much what Bo is thinking.

I know that Bo is actually in the power position. Bo isn't being pushed by the horse on his hip; Bo is leading the horse on his hip. I see the big picture and Bo will too; he's just not quite there yet.

There is another major lesson coming up for both Bo and Swizzle. Right now Bo would like to be able to correct Swizzle by having her move off his hip. Swizzle isn't expecting Bo to react to her at all. She looks only to me for direction. As Bo progresses and matures as a pony horse the day will come when he has proven his obedience to my direction and will understand where the horse being ponied belongs and the rules apply to them both. When Bo is well enough schooled I will begin to delegate some responsibility for correcting the ponied horse to him. To allow Bo to correct Swizzle now would let him turn into a little tyrant. He would not be correcting using my criteria but his own. That would be unfair to Bo and really unfair to Swizzle.

Whether human or horse, young or old, individuals can turn into bullies when they are given authority or are placed in charge prematurely. Tyrants are created when they are given authority without having learned humility, when they rule their subordinates from a strictly selfish, ego-driven motivation.

## A Higher Plan

My plans for Bo are well laid out. Each lesson learned allows us to work on the next one. Bo sees only the lesson we worked on today. Bo has no idea that he will learn to carry me around the arena so I can work another horse on my rope just as if I was on the ground. He will be my partner as we train other horses. My knees are almost shot. Bo has four good legs and will be a "service" horse as well as a working pony. I know Bo will successfully work through each level and become the horse I intend him to be. I also haven't told him that he is going to have to learn to bow so I can get on without a mounting block. He'll do that too. He just can't see it yet.

All my plans for Bo depend on his habit of obedience and my ability to communicate each small step to him in a way he can process. Bo will learn to accept and do what I ask, even if he doesn't understand why I am asking.

All our plans for our children begin this way. All God's plans for us begin this way. You can bet He has the plan all worked out. We can't see the future as He does. We have no idea what the next step will be as we continue growing into the people God planned for each of us to be. Success begins with our habit of obedience, even when we think the current lesson makes no sense.

Bo and Swizzle trust me enough to obey, and I am only a simple human. How silly we are to think that God doesn't know what He's doing. We simply need to calmly, quietly, and happily obey.

# LEADING GROUPS

*The sheep hear his voice; and he calls his own sheep by name and leads them out.*

John 10:3

*The best learning I had came from teaching.*

Corrie Ten Boom

As I described in the previous chapter, the nature of a relationship is tested as soon as an outsider is added to the equation. You may recall that my relationship with Bo was tested when a third party was added to the picture. As obedient as Bo is, when we started ponying Swizzle a relationship triangle was formed and the strength and parameters of my relationship with Bo were tested and found to be in need of reinforcement.

In my opinion, there are two basic ways to lead groups: a military style and a relational style. In the military style, all group members are trained exactly the same. There are negative consequences for any behavior outside that prescribed by the leader. There is no allowance given for individual differences whether physical, mental, aptitude, or preferential. All are judged the same.

The relational style of leading groups is like training horses. The illustration that comes to mind is the multi-horse acts of *Cavalia,* a multimedia stage presentation that showcases the bond between humans and horses. Each horse has to be trained separately until it is so focused on the leader that it will remain obedient when another horse is added. Each successive horse must also be separately trained. Then, the relationship with each horse is tested as they are put together to perform. Corrections must be made individually.

In essence, the horses are not a team; they are performing independently but in unison. When adding additional horses, the procedure remains the same. Each horse must be in a right relationship with the trainer before being added to the act. As each horse needs additional work, it must be separated and weak places strengthened before joining up with the others again.

Horses who work in unison, who are trained in a relational style, never truly work as a team unless there comes a time when they experience the unifying experience of a military style of reward or consequence. It is certainly possible to make great horse teams. Horses will learn incrementally how to hold their position in a multi-horse hitch. Teams learn to pull together, discovering how they can minimize the load when they combine their efforts in synergistic rhythm.

Team spirit and team relationship or connection is made when the members of the team are treated not as individuals, but as parts of a whole. What any member experiences, all members experience. There may be exceptions for gross violations of the rules, but the exception is well understood by others, and there is also a lesson for them as they witness the punishment of the offender. And in the military style of group leadership, consequences are considered and meant as punishments, not as corrections. The culture of an organization or corps determines which type of leadership is most effective or most desired. As one moves up through the ranks in the military from Private to General, the leadership style begins to shift to one that is a mixture of the two styles, and we begin to see more characteristics of relational leadership utilized by superiors.

What is the goal of leadership? The military has a goal with new recruits of instilling a habit, a core allegiance to the mission, the organization, their fellow soldiers, and to pure obedience without question. To accomplish this goal, the leadership style is by necessity (and name) a purely militaristic one.

Not everyone will successfully graduate from military boot camp. The recruit is changed when he begins to live in a group experience. Boot camp teaches these raw soldiers-in-the-making basic lessons of leadership and followership. For military purposes, for the purpose of formulating and successfully waging war, the ability to send a group of men out to work as a single unit is imperative. Anarchy in the troops only leads to casualties and defeat. Independence is death to the fighting man or woman.

How does one best lead a group of leaders?

How does one best lead a group of followers?

The simple rule, which just begs for exceptions of which there are many, is that leaders are led in a mix of military/relational leadership style, trending more toward the relational side of the continuum. Followers are led also by a mixture of the two leadership styles but trend more toward the militaristic side of the spectrum.

Followers want rules. They thrive on the security that boundaries and procedures offer. Rules offer consistency, reliability, clarity, and keep the follower from feeling insecure and out of his depth. Rules offer comfort.

This concept also applies to children. Horses love consistency and routine. Most people prefer consistency and security, though some are more able than others to eventually feel comfortable and secure in a routine of non-routine.

Leaders want the opportunity to step out in front and prove what they can do. They wilt and are repressed by too many boundaries and procedures. And, leaders, by definition, must get out in front. Otherwise they are pushers, not leaders, and the entire dynamic is changed. It has been oft-repeated that, "God leads; Satan pushes." When considering the topic of leadership, this is a concept that the Christian leader must eventually contemplate in order to be effective.

How does one lead a group of leaders in an organization? The process of learning leadership and effective relationship skills is very similar. They are learned through trial and error, by experiencing success and failure. As with many skills or concepts, we learn our greatest lessons through our greatest failures. Leadership is a skill that will generalize to any situation, as is relationship building. What do I mean by generalizing? If you learn to be an effective horse trainer, it means you can train almost any horse, regardless of breed, type, or disposition. Successfully training one horse does not a horse trainer make. Even a person who is famous for being undesirable as a friend or coworker probably has one person with whom he has a successful relationship. He is, however, unable to replicate that skill with other people. A horse trainer must be able to train many horses, not just one.

A leader must be able to lead many types of followers in a variety of situations, not just one little group, one time. They must be able to replicate their leadership success. The same is true of relationship building.

Leadership is more complicated than simply looking at how a couple of basic styles work with different types of groups. There are leaders who are placed in their positions by assuming the directing role of an existing group. An example would be the incoming president of a club. The club membership exists, the rules are in place, and hopefully the new president will be an effective leader. Being effective in this instance means fulfilling the mission of the club utilizing the talents of the membership in a way that enhances both the club and each member. This leader may steer the club in new and more productive directions and achieve higher levels of success than were experienced in the past. Proven leaders are necessary, even when the existing body is already somewhat orderly and effective, otherwise the group will begin to weaken and factionalize. Poor leaders can wipe out the work done by prior excellent leaders if no action is taken to educate or remove them before the damage is irreversible.

There is a completely different leadership model that applies to a leader who attracts and builds a base of followership that did not previously exist. These are very unique people with a skill set not easily taught. Leadership is a skill that can be taught with success to most people. However, not all people will ever be great leaders. Let me attempt to explain the difference using musical talent as an analogy.

In my family, all the talent related to the artistic side of music went to my brother. Some ability to be technically correct fell my way. My brother has perfect pitch, can sing, can play an instrument by ear, and could probably have had some success as a musician. I can't carry a tune from one room to another, but I can read music and apply what is on the page to finger position on piano keys. For a number of years, I served as church organist for a little rural church.

No one else stepped up to play, so the congregation was happy to have me, musical warts and all. I never deceived myself into believing I could play the organ. I just know how to translate a black dot printed on a page to a corresponding finger motion. Had I applied myself and dedicated myself to a serious study of music I could have improved my skills, but no matter what I did, I could never have perfect pitch, be able to sing with anyone but God benefiting, or play by ear. I just don't have the right ears.

What was the trade off? I learned that I could "lead" by ear, that I understood the concepts of relationship building as part of my nature. My early career didn't always benefit from these skills. I had to learn basics, concepts, and how to apply them. Just as the person with perfect pitch feels a natural affinity to music, I feel a natural affinity for relational concepts. Training horses came naturally to me. But it took years of study, failures, successes, and many patient horses to help me further my natural ability and develop skills that now generalize to almost any horse. The perspective I gained from being at the bottom of the stairs looking up in both relationships and groups, as well as that gained from the top of the stairs looking down, has been a vital tool for me. For instance, I learned more about being a successful horse show exhibitor from being a horse show judge than from any other single activity or study.

### The View from the Center of the Arena

For a number of years, I specialized in Halter horses. Fitting and showing halter horses is not the simple matter those who are not in the industry believe it to be. It is nearly as complex as the game of golf. Feeding and exercise programs for young horses often require daily tweaks to keep the immature horse healthy and growing normally. How high one has a horse hold its head when presented to the judge may move it from a first place trophy to a sixth place ribbon. I will never forget the first time I judged a halter class and saw an exhibitor bend over from the waist, backside facing me, to reset a front foot to better present their horse. All well and good, but it was not a pretty picture; the backside, I mean. Realizing that I, too, had made that exact move more than once, I was mortified. Is that what that looked like? I never did it again.

Similar observations came along when I judged other events such as reining, pleasure, hunt seat, or trail. Seeing a performance from the center of the ring is quite a different thing from seeing that same performance from the bleachers or in-gate. You cannot properly judge unless you are the judge. There is a singularity of perspective that cannot be shared with someone standing elsewhere in the arena or building.

In contrast, I believe I was a successful judge because I had first been an exhibitor. The evaluations I received as a judge were nearly always at the highest end of the scale. I became a judge to uniformly and fairly judge exhibitor performance by applying the rulebook and not by political or inappropriately subjective influence.

I will never learn all there is to know about horses or leadership. I suppose that is one reason natural horse trainers can never hang up their snaffle-bit for good, and leaders can never completely retire from people activities. There will always be a higher level of understanding to achieve, a new lesson to learn, and the only way to test our knowledge is by applying it.

Sometimes Christians have difficulty in understanding leadership roles. Are we to judge others? In what circumstances and to what degree? Where do we draw the line between brotherly love and accountability? In some instances, there is great confusion between the idea that "God will provide" and "I am responsible." Accountability is a fundamental element in both leadership and followership. Why, I wonder, do Americans have such a difficult time requiring others to be accountable for their actions? When accountability is removed, leadership disappears, goals are not met, nations may crumble, and God is not served. Nowhere does Scripture teach us to be unaccountable. Several of Jesus Christ's parables speak specifically to accountability.

To sum up, when you lead a group, it is necessary to evaluate the style of leadership that will provide the best result. In most instances, you will use a mixture of both the militaristic and relational styles. We must also develop a relationship with each horse we intend to use in a team. Once the relationship with each horse is well founded, we begin to work them together, each horse eventually learning to do its part of the whole.

God does the same with us. We work with the Spirit to build a right relationship with Him; His leadership being very relational and personal. He is a personal God. However, we all belong to a larger group as children of God, the body of Christ. We are all subject to the same rules and expectations, and as His children we will all be united in our final home—that place with many mansions that Jesus has prepared for us.

# DISTRACTIONS

*Therefore keep watch, because you do not know the day or the hour.*

Matthew 25:13

*If opportunity knocks while you are distracted—what was I saying?*

Unknown

Have you ever watched horses or cattle as they spend an August day in the pasture, grazing on the mature grasses, trying to search out one especially tender green shoot among the taller, tougher blades? If there is shelter available, horses and cattle will spend much of the afternoon under cover or shoulder deep in the water, trying to stay out of the hot sun and away from flies.

When flies are especially bad or the nastiest varieties have made their way to the pasture, horses wear the visual evidence of these tormentors on their bodies. The horses with the thinnest skin will be covered in welts ranging from the size of a mosquito bite to the size of a softball.

Just a few years ago, West Nile Virus became an issue for horse owners as well as humans. The virus is carried by mosquitoes and has a high mortality rate for horses, though less so for humans. Most well cared for horses are now vaccinated annually for West Nile Virus as their owners continue to be vigilant and protect them from pestilence. Are you that concerned with the safety of your own family?

What books are lurking in the back row of that bookcase upstairs in the junk room? What old videos are tucked away in the box on your closet floor? Exactly what music is forgotten in the attic or stored on each iPod or MP3 player in your home? What magazines are tucked under your teenager's mattress? What Web sites have your children been visiting when they retire to their bedrooms for the night? Who are they chatting with on the worldwide Web?

Where are the pests and varmints lurking in your home? In your spirit? Every wrong book, every wrong video, every wrong Internet search opens another portal for evil to enter your home or for righteousness to leave. Does the way you dress matter? What you read? The music you listen to? What you watch on television? The answer to all of these questions is yes.

These are, at the very least, distractions from the work necessary to build a right relationship to God and, at the worst, direct assaults by the enemy against the work of the Spirit. Until January of 2008, I used to take the last few minutes before I fell asleep to read the Bible and do my devotions. I struggled with my understanding, wondering if I was in need of special education. Well, we are all in need of special education and the good news is it is there for the taking. The obvious question I should have been asking myself is whether my difficulties were the result of an inability or unwillingness. My answer at the time would probably have been inability.

However, now that I have been promoted to a higher grade, I know that what I kept stumbling over was unwillingness. Over the years I had indulged in intellectual pursuit of knowledge about parapsychology, the spiritual, and the experiences of Christians who reported near-death experiences. I was never into anything other than pure discovery, trying to add to my understanding of God and where people fit into the realms beyond our sight. I have the basic disposition of a researcher, so I figured I was being curious and thoughtful in this pursuit. In truth, my relationship with the Lord was handicapped by my disobedience to His Word and the distractions and opportunities for evil that came in with my study materials.

God addresses this issue directly in His Word. Why I had failed to grasp its meaning until now is a mystery, yet now it was finally revealed—or I had finally cleared out enough distractions to allow me to properly diagnose my issue of unwillingness. Is there spiritual activity we can't see? Yes, but Christians are not to play in that arena. We are to inquire only of God, not of those who have already died or of spiritual beings who never had human form. Adam and Eve were told to stay away from the tree of knowledge. We are told to stay away from all sources of information outside the earthly realm other than those provided directly by the Lord for His purposes. Knowledge, in and of itself, is not virtuous, nor is all knowledge inherently healthy. The pursuit of knowledge outside of that which is rightly ours only adds to the mountain of distractions we must fight to remove in order to find a right relationship with God. I had to learn to be content and to inquire only of the Lord for supernatural understanding and leave the rest alone.

Two things changed. The influence of our Bible study group finally allowed me to hear the quiet voice of the Spirit. I stopped giving the Lord the last little bit I had left every day and began giving the first and best of my day to Him. Should this come as a surprise to any of us that we are to give the first fruits to the Lord? The concept of tithing, taking a portion off the top, is biblical and has been presented to us repeatedly, usually without proper effect. The story of the Lord begins in Genesis, and the concept of giving of what we have to the Lord makes its debut in chapter 4. My Bible has 2,624 pages of actual Scripture; this most basic element of right relationship appears on the ninth page. What does this mean to you about its relative importance?

The Lord looked with favor on the offering of Abel, not so with Cain, who got pretty sullen and unhappy about the situation. In Genesis 4:6–7, God asks Cain, "Why are you angry? Why is your face downcast? If you do what is right, will you not be accepted? But if you do not do what is right, sin is crouching at your door; it desires to have you, but you must master it." Well, you all know what happened next.

Having now figured out (I didn't say I was a quick study) that I needed to give the beginning of each day to God rather than the remnant, the Spirit opened my eyes and ears to His teaching as I had never experienced before. What a blessing!

The second thing that changed was my recognizing the vulnerable openings I had left for evil to come in, the opportunity for distractions to enter my home. I sat in my chair one morning having prayed, read my Chambers and the scripture of the day. After these basics, each day I follow the lead of the Spirit. One day I was "in school" and I was very pointedly reminded that I still had a few of the books in my upstairs bookcase written by Christians who had near-death experiences. I had all but forgotten they were even up there. Talk about convicted!

I immediately got up and went to that bookcase. I pulled each and every one of those books out and flung them into the trashcan in the garage ready for pick up the next morning. I had never waited so impatiently for the garbage truck as I did that day. In my mind, I ran through everything else I could think of that might possibly give opening to any spirit other than the holiest. Immediately the books were gone, I felt lighter in spirit than I had ever before. I returned to my chair, chastened and ashamed. My teacher had patiently waited for my return. He gave me a warm "hug" of approval and continued the day's lesson.

In the entry of our home is a sign quoting Joshua 24:15. For those of you who can't immediately remember it, the verse is, "But as for me and my house, we will serve the Lord."

There is to be nothing in our home that provides a stumbling block to that service. Not one thing. Not a television show, a magazine, music, or even a catalog. Is it really necessary to be so picky about what we allow into our homes? Well, does it bother you when just one persistent fly keeps after you, landing first on your hand, then on your nose, then on your sandwich, then on your ear...?

It drives you nuts! Do you think God cares less about that one small, irritating object that you refuse to part with than you do that tiny little fly? There are many things we allow in our lives that are not evil but that create situations that cause you way more work as you fight to keep distractions under control. Let me share a story from the barn with you. See how it might open your eyes to similar situations in your life and home.

When I was fitting halter horses in Arizona, we cooked "dessert" for them each day. Oats were boiled for two hours each afternoon. Once the cooked oats and broth cooled, I added bran and dried molasses, stirring up the equivalent of a hot fudge sundae. The slop (as we called it) was the highlight of the horses' day, and they nickered and begged until they were able to shove their eager faces down into their buckets of sweet oats and soup. We called the warm mash slop because the noise made by the horses as they happily smacked their way through their dessert reminded us of the noise made by hogs in slop. The mash had lots of juice with the oats and created happy, sticky, pony faces.

When we moved to Texas, we continued cooking oats and serving dessert to the barn horses in the cooler months. It didn't take too long before we began having a serious fly problem. The automatic fly system was no longer holding off the hordes of annoying pests. I had never experienced such a challenge. At that time, if I found three flies in my barn in one day, I prepared for war. There was just no keeping ahead of the flies, and I could not figure it out. I had never had to resort to fly spray directly on the horses in the barn and also got out flysheets and masks. What I discovered was that flies just love slop. The molasses drew them like, well…like flies.

We cleaned each bucket daily, but just the remnant of the soup kept them coming. Sadly, we quit cooking for the horses. This is an example of a distraction that is not of itself a bad thing. Quite the opposite, in fact. However, the extra work and annoyance caused by the flies exceeded the benefit we received, and slop is now just a fond memory. I must say I don't miss the extra work, but I do miss the delight my horses took in this wonderful treat. Nobody misses the flies.

## Neighbors Are Part of Your Environment

When training horses, it is important to control the environment as much as possible to reduce the distraction caused by the simple irritation of flies or the greater problem of biting insects that break the concentration of the horse (and rider), making learning difficult or impossible. In order to keep our horses comfortable and able to learn, we need to prevent these pests from invading our space. Flies and insects can be far more harmful than the obvious issues of nagging and distraction. Horses will rub and scratch the itchy places caused by insect bites even to the point of destroying their manes and tails or opening great cuts and sores as they try to find relief.

Actual irritants and discomforts make our horses unable to get the most out of each lesson. On one hand, we limit the value of our training time if we allow flies to distract. On the other hand, not controlling mosquitoes can cause more than simple bites and rubs; mosquitoes can kill if they carry West Nile Virus.

You need to manage the distractions, and varmints, which affect you, your soul, and your family. It greatly matters with whom you associate and with whom your children spend their time. There are good influences, and there are bad influences. There are environmental factors that are dismissed as inconsequential when in fact they have great impact on the spiritual health of you and your family. What do you allow in your home that offers a gateway to the enemy? You can no more keep your home in a proper condition for the Spirit to work efficiently than you can keep the hot summer winds from coming in through openings in poorly fitting doors and windows.

Your air conditioner will work much harder to keep your house cool when it is not properly sealed than it would otherwise. The costs to you of drafty and poorly insulated homes are increased utility bills, less comfort, and a way bigger need to dust daily to remove the dirt blown in through cracks and crevices. The cost to you of unguarded access to your home and spirit-life is the degree to which you can be rightly related to God.

It absolutely matters with whom you associate, who your neighbors are, and what they do. You can keep the cleanest barn in the state, have a built-in fly system that regularly sprays your stalls and pens, serve feed-through products to your animals to kill larvae on manure piles, and even release fly predators to kill the ones you missed through your other efforts. However, if the guy next door has a horse, a cow, or a goat, and does not wage war against his flies to the same extent you do, his flies will be more than happy to come visit your lovely place.

Many times over the years I have been asked by new horse owners to suggest ways to help them control their fly problem. I always begin by asking about the neighborhood. Fly control is expensive. If your neighbor isn't concerned about his fly problem, you have a much shorter list of options for controlling yours.

**Be Ruthless**

What can you do? Be vigilant. Be aware. Be obedient. God will watch over you, your horses, and your family while you sleep. During the day, however, He expects you to seal the spiritual leaks in your home, monitor what is heard and seen by your family, and keep distractions to the lowest level possible. Be ruthless as you clear out questionable material from your house.

Is this responsibility easy? No. Is it fair? The relationships you enjoy with your horse, your children, and with God are not democracies. These relationships are blessings. Horse owners plan for the protection of their horses from irritating and destructive pests. It is expensive, time consuming, and a constant battle from early spring till late fall. It takes planning and commitment. Would you do less for your home and family? For yourself?

Identify everything and anything that distracts you from the blessing of right relationship with the Lord. Remember, just one tiny fly can consume your attention. Open your home to God, but close it tightly against the distractions and filth of the enemy. Give God the first and best of your day. Clean house. Let the fresh, healing breezes of the Holy Spirit move into your home, your spirit, and your life.

# CORRECTION, NOT PUNISHMENT

*O Lord, correct me, but with judgment.*

Jeremiah 10:24

*Correction is not for the detection of faults, but in order to make perfect... Our wills must share in the making; God does not make us good in spite of ourselves. Those who take God's way of coming into the light will find, ultimately, nothing but unspeakable joy and peace, life and love.*

Oswald Chambers

The differences that matter most between correction and punishment are ones of intent and goal. Punishment is used to confront, to dominate the one being punished. The goal of punishment is to stop a particular unwanted or dangerous behavior.

Correction is used in order to improve or make perfect. The goal of correction is to encourage right behavior. The actual visual picture of punishment and correction may look the same to the uninformed, but the one on the receiving end certainly knows the difference.

Some horses are cinchy; they get angry whenever the girth begins to pull close around their belly. These horses aren't reacting because the design of the saddle and girth are incorrect but because the hands that apply them are inept, arrogant, cruel, or ignorant. Most horses learn to willingly accept the metal bit and snug saddle when they are introduced correctly.

Too many times trainers or horse owners resort to bigger bits and tighter girths to correct a horse's response or because the saddle doesn't fit correctly. Bigger bits are only properly used with increasingly lighter cues until the horse and rider move as one, with no visible method of communication. The pair appears to be united psychically, no longer tied to the merely physical. Severe bits or "enhanced training equipment" are wrongly used by trainers or owners to dominate horses by inflicting pain when trainers want to achieve faster results or when an owner has exhausted his or her library of knowledge and resorts to simple brutality.

Many times in my training career I tied a horse's head around by a (snaffle) rein to the stirrup or girth ring. Was this punishment or correction? I always used it as a means for the horse to teach itself. The rein was never so tight that the horse couldn't find the right answer and be completely comfortable. My goal was to teach the horse to give to pressure. I haven't done this for quite a while now, as there are other methods I much prefer. However, when I had a whole string of horses to train, I wasn't able to spend as much time with each one as I am now. As a trainer, I was paid to get results. The horse's safety and welfare were always of utmost concern to me, but if I could have one horse in the round pen teaching himself, I could be riding another horse in the adjacent arena, always keeping an eye on the one tied around.

Tying a horse around is a method of putting the horse in a bind until they figure the way out on their own. This exercise must be done with judgment, wisdom, and under constant observation or it may quickly become an act of cruelty.

Have you ever found yourself in a bind? When the Lord puts us in a bind with judgment and His wisdom, we can be sure we are never left unobserved and His plans always include the opportunity for us to learn to find the right answer that will give us release. He may leave us to figure it out on our own for a time, but never in true peril. Horses remember more quickly when they have reasoned out answers on their own. So do humans.

Is there ever a circumstance where leaving a horse tied in a bind doesn't work? Absolutely. Not all people learn the same way, and all horses don't either. Few things are as frustrating to the good horse trainer as a horse who is put into a bind, be it ever so slight, and he simply will not look for a way to relieve the pressure. Pressure can be slowly and systematically increased in an attempt to find the spot where the horse feels the need to work on figuring a way out of his problem. For some horses, there is no place between dead stop and explode. The good trainer knows when to abandon such exercises and try another approach before the horse gets anywhere close to explode, which exposes it to injury or worse.

Warning: never tie a rope or rein hard and fast to you or your horse unless you know what you are doing!

How God must be frustrated with men when He finds one like the horse who simply will not try. He tries to teach us using subtle pressure. Instead of recognizing our situation, we persist in inaction until He is forced to change the program. His application of pressure, however slight, is meant to teach us. When we simply refuse to even try, He may increase our bind slowly and methodically until we either learn or explode. Some people just never learn and are in danger of being washed out of His training program completely.

There are, unfortunately, many trainers and riders who apply correction without wisdom or judgment. The examples are so numerous I have difficulty separating out only one.

### The Noble Youth Horse

As a horse show judge, one of the rider errors that most irritated me occurred during youth trail classes. How many times did young riders bang their horses in the mouth with a correction bit or jab them in the side with a sharp-roweled spur when a trail obstacle was poorly performed? I cannot count the number of occasions. To be fair, there were also plenty of adult riders in this group of bad actors. Memories are flooding into my mind of instances where the exhibitor was an adult, or worse yet, a trainer, who "corrected" his horse in a similar way.

My frustration in these cases wasn't generated by the severity of the correction but the fact that correction was absolutely not justified. The poor performances were not a result of the horse's refusal, confusion, sloppiness, or disobedience. My irritation was that in each instance, the horse had obediently done exactly as the rider had asked. The errors were caused by the rider 100 percent of the time. Yet the poor horse was the one who received the punishment.

During the years I did most of my judging, the rulebooks didn't include specific rules penalizing this behavior. As a judge, I did have discretion to use my opinion of how well each obstacle was performed; judging correctness, style, and substance. I penalized riders each and every time they used their horse as a whipping boy, dishing out punishment to the poor horse when the rider deserved the blame. The pulling and poking applied by these kids never rose to the level of abuse, or I would have thrown them out of the arena. Nonetheless, these horses endured punishment for absolutely no good reason.

I cannot tell you how many times I've said, "I have no idea why such horses don't just reach around and grab these kids, drop them in the dirt, stomp 'em, and walk away." Yet those youth horses took what the little monsters dished out without complaint. Did those horses refuse to retaliate out of fear or from nobility? How difficult it is to understand why an 1,100-pound animal would patiently submit to undeserved punishment for the bad behavior of the 95-pound kid on its back. Any time they wanted to those horses could have ditched their kids and left the arena. They never did.

Even now, I feel respect, admiration, and affection for those wonderful youth horses. Until now I never noticed the similarity of the behavior of these horses to the mortification of Jesus Christ. Jesus was sinless, yet He quietly endured punishment—unto death—for our bad behavior. At any time during His passion, Jesus could have ditched Pilate and the errant Jews and left the scene of His torment. He did not. How can we wrap our minds around such sacrifice? It wasn't fair. The guilty (us) got off without punishment.

I still don't know what causes youth horses to patiently endure punishment, not just for crimes they did not commit, but enduring punishment applied by the very ones who are themselves guilty. The only explanation seems to be in the similarity and simplicity of horses. Like God, horses treat us exactly as we deserve - unless they bless us with grace.

Similar stories of horses receiving undeserved punishment in the name of correction are repeated over and over daily in the horse world. On behalf of all the horses and all my Christian brethren, I pray, as did Jeremiah, "O Lord, correct me, but with judgment."

Will every horse respond as hoped to judicially applied correction, even correction that is appropriate, intended to improve, to make perfect, and done with a goal of encouraging the right behavior? Can we make every horse behave well in spite of its resistance? No, we cannot. The horse's will is part of the equation and must be involved in the work of making perfect. The horse that learns to learn, that accepts the trainer as a leader who offers a wonderful relationship, is the horse who finds security and confidence, a full manger, warm stall, and affection.

So it is with Christians. We begin to respond to God; we accept Jesus Christ as our personal Savior, who offers us the most wonderful relationship that surpasses our imagination. As long as we continue to experience correction, we may be confident that we remain in training, still actively pursuing relationship with God. When we accept God's way, we come into the light, ultimately finding nothing but unspeakable joy and peace, life, and love.

# I AM THE HORSE

*I do what I don't will, and what I will I don't do.*

Romans 7:19

*God's commands are designed to guide you to life's very best. You will not obey Him, if you do not believe in Him and trust Him. You cannot believe Him if you do not love Him. You cannot love Him unless you know Him.*

Dr. Henry Blackaby

As I write this I realize how confusing the past two days have been. I have been ashamed and I have backslid in my walk with the Lord as it involves my work. The work began to take on an importance of its own. I thought I was becoming important in my own right again. Wrong!

Thankfully, I was able to go to the Lord, and as He is ever faithful, He corrected me and gave me a way to truly understand what my role is and what it is not. God has clarified for me, again, what I am to do and why. I needed to be slapped down and sent back into obedience training. The Lord was easier on me than I was on myself. He let me know I had not sinned but I had become somewhat untrained. Yet He welcomed me back and provided the moral to my lesson. On this issue of arrogance I require regular maintenance.

Yesterday Baber and I took Copper and Bo to a Texas Smokin' Guns competition. My work has been taking more time than in the past, and I have been devoting less regular time to my relationships with Bo and Swizzle. Trying to cheat our quality time...

At the shoot, Bo was not his usual obedient self. There was a balloon crew, so Bo and I did not run sticks much. I missed the opportunity to refresh Bo's habit of obedience in a warm-up as we had been doing. Copper was okay but stiffer than he needed to be and way too emotional, though not to any serious degree. After two poor stages, with Bo offering some resistance and a bit of his own opinion on what we should do, it became obvious that his habit of obedience needed some maintenance. Why in the world was Bo concerned about that rusty barrel lying in the trees one hundred feet away? And why was he throwing his head up to become a breathing statue just because there were cattle lazily moving across the pasture on the far side of the road? When I got on Copper the first time, he refused to walk through a two-inch-deep depression. What? It took fifteen minutes of exercises to get Copper to obediently go back and forth through the rut in the road without hesitating or refusing. So take comfort, all you horse people. We all have days like this.

I was able to work both Bo and Copper through their lack of obedience because I had lots of foundation to work with. I lunged each with their halter and lead rope at a trot, frequently asking them to turn from just the direction of my hand and a gentle feel in the lead rope. As each mastered the exercise, they also changed from reactive back to thinking, from independence to obedience. Our rides afterwards were exactly as they should be.

This morning it occurred to me that yesterday was really a lesson intended for me. Bo and Copper did to me what I had done to God the week before. In our routine at home, my grays remain obedient with very little maintenance. I, too, stay focused more easily without the extra distractions of being out in public. But when you take me out to a "show", put me in another environment, especially one where I am used to shining, well, not so much. It took the trainer in me to recognize the issue with Bo and Copper and work the fix. The trainer in me also recognized how I had come untrained and what fix was necessary to correct my own behavior. Praise God I was blessed with these amazing horses. Today, I realized how I had failed to keep myself maintained in daily obedience.

In my relationship with God, I am the horse; He is both owner and trainer, the best trainer. God knew me before He selected my parents, claimed me at birth, and has cared for me all my life. He sent me out at the appropriate time for basic training. There was never a time when He was not in control of my program and each apprentice-trainer who worked with me was never left unsupervised. As I progressed and excelled, He sent me out to practice shows and ultimately as a proven champion, though I have certainly never achieved world champion status in His work.

Last October He brought me back to His barn. I came home to be His "horse" for training to do His work.

Just because I have a nice record as a show horse doesn't mean God will ever take me to show again. Indeed, only He knows whether or not I will ever perform again for another's judgment. This is not a waste of my talent or ability. He cares for me. I am only required to be obedient, and the degree to which I commit to our relationship determines the degree to which I am elevated in His opinion and favor.

Yes, I look good with a full show clip, but such specific grooming is no longer very important to Him. I don't have to be show ready to serve His purpose. He prefers me in a mostly natural state unless I am to be slicked up to represent Him in an arena of His choice. I stay fit and healthy for my own benefit, but also to be ready whenever I may be called to work. Indeed, as a show horse I was clipped to exhibit a standard of appearance He may never choose again. In fact, I am safer in most environments with some of my "whiskers" left in their natural state. He designed me well.

God has provided me with a wonderful barn (home), beautiful pasture (community), and a circle of friends (my herd.) When He has no immediate need of me, I am free to play, exercise, eat, relate to my herd, and make my own choices. I am always to have an ear cocked in His direction, listening for His footsteps, waiting for His call. When God wants me, I wish to be immediately ready and come at the speed He requests. How frustrating it is to call a horse in from the pasture, asking it to show up quickly and waiting while it merely ambles along in our direction. I do not want to keep Him waiting for my arrival when I am called. That would not the best start of any assignment.

There is much schooling left to do. Most of my training is done at home in private. He takes me out to test our relationship to determine how well I have learned my lessons. My skills are to be available to Him at the time and place of His choosing. God keeps me maintained; faithful to provide fine tuning when needed for a specific, precise task.

At times I may be used as a leader to show a more timid "horse" the way, or as a pony horse to guide another in a loose partnership, but always directed by my Leader. God chooses when, He chooses whom, and He chooses where. I am no longer a full-time show horse. I am still capable, but that is not His plan as far as I see it. Now, I am the beloved friend, companion, partner, and obedient horse of my Master who has promised to value and cherish me forever.

Relationship is all that truly matters. Everything else is merely window dressing.

# PRETTY IS AS PRETTY DOES

*He had no beauty or majesty to attract us to him, nothing in his appearance that we should desire him. He was despised and rejected by men.*

Isaiah 53:2-3

*Do you love me because I'm beautiful, or am I beautiful because you love me?*

Oscar Hammerstein II

An overnight internet sensation, Susan Boyle, 47, not a beauty by any traditional standards, stunned the world in April 2009 in a British talent competition with her rendition of "I Dreamed a Dream" from *Les Miserables*. The three-judge panel was at first highly skeptical, then enraptured, when she opened her mouth and the beauty of her song filled the theatre.

How many people are outwardly beautiful yet inwardly corrupt? How can it be that such beauty, talent, innocence, even naiveté, resides in a woman who looked like Susan Boyle at this audition?

How does our world view a Susan Boyle? It depends on what eyes we use to see her. If we use the eyes of a corrupted people, we discount Susan's gift; we see little, if any, beauty. Indeed, we wish her to leave the stage so one more attractive than she may enter the spotlight. With such ignorant eyes, we are repulsed by the unexpected contrast between the physical and the vocal, demanding that someone more acceptable replace this one.

However, if we look with eyes of righteousness, with eyes that are still able to see what lies beneath the veneer, we are elevated by the gift of Susan Boyle—not only her song, but also her innocence. We are captivated. How could such a talent remain unseen for so many years? Susan lived a life of service to her parents. She did not attempt to venture into the limelight until this competition.

In today's society, the greater part of value is in the physical, in youth, in celebrity, in all that fades and is no more than dust when we pass on. What is wrong with us? I asked a friend of mine when we first discovered Susan Boyle, if she had the opportunity to receive Susan's gift, but a requisite was that she also would have Susan's appearance, what would she choose? Would it be beauty of face and form or an amazing beauty of spirit and song? I was surprised that my friend answered with little hesitation; she would accept the physical to obtain the spiritual. Mind you, my friend is a very attractive lady. If I asked myself the same question, what answer would I give? I don't know. What answer would you give?

What I do know is that while I am truly not inclined to exchange my life for anyone else's, I realize that I am in error frequently about how I conduct my own. Why is it that I am concerned about the wrinkles spreading across my face? Why do I look at photographs of myself twenty or thirty years ago and feel like I am somehow failing because I do not look the same?

Any meaningful beauty I have to offer will not be physical. The only true beauty is the spiritual beauty given to me through my relationship to Jesus Christ. Such beauty can only be visible to others if I am oblivious to it. There's the difficulty. I know that. I want spiritual beauty. I also want physical beauty. I was used to having it. So, what is my bottom line?

I want to be obedient to the Lord. The only way I can obtain the relationship I want with Him is to be willing to lose myself so I may become what the Spirit can make me. What is the lesson we learn from Susan Boyle? The sensation she caused is due to the childlike affect she brings married to the phenomenal beauty of her song, which is in such stark contrast to her appearance. What is the result? Her appearance begins to take on an external beauty caused by her inner radiance. Will she have a complete makeover of the external? Would a makeover lessen the package? God has brought her to this place. May she remain true to the beauty she came with. May I work to have an inner beauty that transforms my exterior in the same way Susan's has been.

## You Can't Ride Beauty

Most horse trade publications these days contain articles on the state of the economy, specifically horse markets and all related industries. An emerging direction in horse values favors horses that already have good job skills. Values of horses have always revolved around these three corners of the market triangle: potential, appearance, and utility. The relative weight of each is rapidly changing as economic realities and markets shift. For years, market demand drove the value of potential to higher and higher levels as breeding numbers were increased and the price of good, then great, broodmares and yearlings kept skyrocketing. Potential was king of the marketplace, bringing in the dominant share of the bids at auction.

There has always been value placed on proven winners, but the older the horse, the smaller the pool of interested buyers seemed to be. Once a performance horse exceeds the age of nomination or eligibility to major money competitions, its value begins to nosedive. In the casual riders market, young never had the value-added status it did in the performance horse market, so it was no surprise that the values for mature casual market horses remained steady but never reached the fever pitch of the cutting, reining, western pleasure and racing markets. Beauty and potential were what was selling. What is selling today?

Today, the potential corner of the market triangle is not bringing the return it was just a couple of years ago. Breeding numbers are, thankfully, going down as market demand rapidly ebbs. A growing trend is the increasing value being placed on seasoned horses that are well established in their occupations, whether casual riding, roping, barrels, competitive trail, or many others. The dressage and eventing communities have long placed a high value on maturity and proven ability. A recent horse sale owned and managed by a well-respected and successful auction company had as its high-selling horse an unregistered palomino pony that was well seasoned in ranch work and the care of children. That pony sold for more than some yearling colts, who just a couple of years ago would have sold for twenty times what the pony did. Potential isn't king of the auction ring anymore.

It is well said that beauty is in the eye of the beholder. If you were buying a prospective mount for your five-year-old granddaughter, would you choose the flashy five-year-old pony that still has obedience issues or the faithful and patient fifteen-year-old pony that at first glance isn't much of a beauty? I hope you would put the fifteen-year-old in your trailer to take home to the waiting stall and your eager granddaughter. Once that pony and your granddaughter have established a relationship, that plain little pony will truly become the most beautiful horse on God's earth.

Spirit transforms us from the inside. This is what a relationship with God is all about. So, what do we learn from Susan Boyle? I learned that I would rather be the plain old pony, beloved by my mistress, than the flashy pony that is not yet fit for a right relationship with any master. As the plain old pony, I am assured of a loving, permanent home where Spirit eyes see my beauty clearly.

# RELATIONSHIP, THE GREATEST BLESSING

*The Lord is my light and my salvation. One thing I have desired of the Lord, that will I seek: that I may dwell in the house of the Lord all the days of my life.*

Psalm 27:1,4

*Life is relationships; the rest is just details.*

Dr. Gary Smalley

When we sold our ranch we built a new house and much smaller horse set-up on one of our hayfields. For the first time in many years, we could see everything we own from anywhere on the place. There are no longer remote fields to hay a mile or more from the house or cattle that graze in a pasture out of sight of the main buildings. The new barn is so close we can see our way to the door of the tack room after dark just by turning on the back porch light. Over the years I have built show barns and barns with stalls used mostly for foaling. I have both remodeled barns and designed barns from scratch. This is the first time I have designed a barn strictly to house our personal horses. This barn will not see horses come in from other people for training, boarding, or foaling. It is only for our little herd, just four stalls.

Convenience and comfort were my primary considerations in the design. Well, economy was also involved, as this barn was a pure expense and not a business investment. But I still wanted my horses housed in a light, airy environment where they have a lot of access to each other, simple but adequate feed storage, a big enough tack room without being expansive, and completely covered, attached runs so we never have to clean manure out of the mud again. The back of each horse's stall/pen combo opens directly into the big back pasture.

In addition to ease of use, one of my highest priorities for the whole place was *low maintenance*. We are not as young as we once were, and I have little interest in "stuff." All that we have been blessed with has the responsibility of good stewardship attached. "To whom much is given, much is expected." Baber and I have been divesting ourselves of stuff for years. My rule for stuff is, "If I don't need it or I don't love it, I don't want it."

My horses are pets again for the first time in nearly twenty years. During most of my equine career, horses were either breeding stock, bred to sell, owned by clients, or horses purchased for eventual resale. Even the few that I claimed as my own over the years weren't really pets. They all had jobs and a purpose. I certainly didn't have time to develop the depth of relationship with any of them that I have now. I have always loved horses, but horses became my job. Just like that proverbial cobbler who had no time to make shoes for his own children, I didn't have the time to concentrate on my own horses. Indeed, as a trainer, my loyalty had to be to my clients. Occasionally, I had to leave our horses at home when we traveled to a horse show, knowing that my horse would likely place higher than a client's horse. That would have been a messy situation and not very professional.

## Chili Bean

Sometimes we don't know what we have until we lose it. Sometimes we don't realize what we don't have until we find it. This particular story is like the latter. About six months before we moved off the ranch to our new place, I lost my dog. Chili Bean had been my baby for nearly fifteen years. Chili, a red miniature dachshund, was one of the special ones. She understood English, and our relationship was a complete blessing to me. Chili had been my most faithful and understanding companion in every situation, even protecting all our belongings one night at a major horse show when thieves broke in to the tack rooms. Little Chili was a true dachshund in many ways, an avid hunter and ready to defend her family's stuff. The special horses and special dogs that bless our lives are those who know our thoughts before we do, who happily give 110 percent of themselves to us. Chili was more than a dog. It was difficult to lose her. Those of you who have been through similar situations know what I felt.

For weeks, each day had begun with the same question, "Is this the day?" Chili was getting less able to find a comfortable position. We gave her pain medication and steroids, but she continued to deteriorate. Finally, the medication was not enough. Chili was in pain constantly. The day I dreaded had finally come. When I returned home from the vet's office that day, I entered the house alone. I was truly unprepared for the void created by Chili's absence. We still had four dogs in the house, yet the life had somehow gone out of it. The heart of my home had stopped beating. My home was now only a house.

My husband mourned Chili's loss deeply. God was still on His throne. Yet, I had no "home," just a house. There was no horse in the barn I could go to who would understand if I went out and woefully hugged its neck.

None of the dogs understood or could comfort me. Baber understood; he is an amazing critter daddy, but he is an autonomous adult man. He doesn't need me to make a home for him. I had never experienced this before. My beloved dachshund-child, Snooker, had passed away in 1990. Snooker deserves a story all her own, but not here. Her passing was worse than Chili's in some ways, but when Snooker passed away, I did have a horse in the barn that was willing and able to provide the comfort I needed. My horse and I had a relationship that reassured me that I was still needed to make him a "home."

It is only now, as I write this, that I understand the process of these losses. There can be very dry periods in our lives, devoid of those rich, special relationships. The empty places remain until a right relationship fills it. Only in hindsight does God explain them to us. We may be comforted always that He has a plan. We cannot understand the plan as it is unfolding, but He is faithful to bring us to understanding at the proper time.

The first morning without Chili was quiet and still. There was still no heartbeat in the house. What an odd situation I found myself in. There was no one in my life that needed me to make a home. The sense of abandonment and uselessness was like sensory deprivation, where your ties to reality are shredded. I had no problem with reality but felt that I was set adrift without a firm tether to a home. That condition continued until yesterday.

### Love Was Born in a Stable

As the Lord walked me through the work of this book, He expanded my understanding of the relationships I have both with Him and with my horses. The blessing of relationship with Jesus Christ is the foundation of my soul and the joy of my life. I am blessed with a husband with whom I am evenly yoked; the comforts we enjoy, and the freedom to live as we prefer; the family and friends we hold so dear. I thought there could be no greater blessing to be reached—at least as far as earthly relationships go.

Yesterday began as a beautiful spring day in north central Texas—sunny, breezy, and warm. Baber and I went out to the barn after getting our inside chores and study done. We curried more of the shedding hair off our horses. I groomed Bo and Swizzle while he groomed Copper and Asti. We saddled all four horses and enjoyed wonderful rides. The clear, sunny day was one of the perfect ones. All four horses learned something new in their lessons, as did we. When all the horses were brushed up and turned back out to the pasture, Baber and I headed off separately to do other projects.

As is not atypical in north central Texas, this spring day that began with brilliant sun and warm breezes changed quickly. The wind began to howl—I mean at gale force levels. The sun was replaced with thick, dark clouds, and the warm balmy day was fast becoming a cold, gusty, winter evening. Temperatures were expected to drop below freezing later that evening. Late in the afternoon I went to the barn. Temperatures had already dropped into the low forties with winds gusting to forty miles per hour. As soon as the horses saw me leave the house, they galloped to the barn and wanted in to their stalls! I asked them to be patient as I added fresh shavings to each stall, checked waterers, and placed large flakes of grass hay into each feeder. Even though the four horses desperately wanted in, they entered their houses in orderly fashion, being just as polite and as patient as they had to be.

The wind was howling as the temperature continued to fall. My horses were so happy to be inside. All were well into the shedding process, and I debated whether or not to put blankets on them. The three older horses hadn't worn a blanket in the two years since we moved, and they became semi-pasture horses. Swizzle, the youngest, had never worn a blanket.

I made my decision. My horses were not going to be cold. Sure, they could take the cold; they were in the barn. But they are precious to me, and I am responsible for their care and I delight in making them secure and comfortable. Out came the blankets. I had to really brush up one or two of them to get the dust of two years off. Clean blankets are folded and stored neatly in sealed plastic bags, but these blankets had been worn a few times right before we moved and had not been cleaned and bagged since, just folded and stored in the tack room. They had never been wet or dirty, just dusty where the odd end or strap had been exposed.

The three older horses eagerly ducked their heads into the neck openings of their blankets. Swizzle had never worn a blanket, and the one I had for her had no opening at the front, so the only way to get it on her was over her head. It took only a few minutes for her to learn about clothes. Once all four were tucked cozily into their jammies and clean, fresh stalls, I went back to the house. At dinner time, I went to the barn to give my little ponies a big flake of alfalfa hay, picked their stalls, and made sure the blankets were all still in place. All was quiet, peaceful, and strangely satisfying.

The next morning was a complete opposite of that first morning without Chili. Somehow I felt my joy expanded beyond normal limits. I felt greatly blessed. Life seemed to be somehow bigger today than it was yesterday. What had happened?

The blessing of relationship. I realized I was needed again as a homemaker. My grays had stepped up to more than meet me halfway in our relationship. The absolute delight I felt as I prepared the barn to ensure the comfort and safety of my horses was totally unexpected. My home had a heartbeat again! Love was born, again, in a stable.

My limited skills as a writer do not allow me to describe what such relationship means. I know that God used this experience as both a blessing and a lesson for me. Our lives can go along in an orderly, contented manner, without our even knowing what we are missing without such relationships. Once we have experienced them, however, we are never truly satisfied until we find them again.

God created us to be in relationship with Him. There is a part of our souls, our hearts, which will always be empty unless filled with Him. There is no other relationship that can take the place reserved for God alone. Once you taste relationship with Him the empty place begins to fill. In John 14, Jesus promises to prepare a place just for us. There is a place with your name on it today, a relationship with Jesus Christ that will forever fill that empty place. He has also prepared a place just for you when you go home to Him. I know the joy I received preparing a place for Bo and Swizzle. Imagine how much more Jesus has done in the place He has prepared exclusively for you.

# PROGRESSIVE RELATIONSHIP

*Because you have kept my command to persevere, I also will keep you from the hour of trial, which shall come upon the whole world.*

Revelation 3:10

*This is the humanist dilemma. They say, "You come from nothing and you're going to nothing, but in between you have great significance." It doesn't make sense at all.*

Pastor Ray Pritchard

The pressure and correction the good trainer applies to her horse is never an element of the specific lesson but rather the result of the horse's failure to comply with, or obey, a request or expectation. Oswald Chambers writes of a similar circumstance Israel found itself in as written in the book of Jeremiah. Chambers says that in Jeremiah, "the prophet realizes that the sufferings and the judgments that are about to fall on the people of God are not a Divine edict, but the result of that people's revolt." In other words, they brought it all on themselves.

When we accept self-realization as the law ruling our life it becomes the enemy of relationship with God. Similarly, a horse's desire to remain outside of the responsibility of a relationship with the good trainer is the very independence that becomes the enemy to the life and success of the relationship. Taken to its ultimate end, if no reversal is made, the relationship ends.

As it is between trainer and horse, so it is between God and man. All of the efforts and worldly propaganda that preach self-love, a turning inward and away from God, is the enemy of a right relationship. The prevailing message in the media today, and throughout much of society, is the worship of humanity.

The lie of Darwin's theory of evolution is but one example of this propaganda. These lies are used to put forth a particular point of view or belief system. It is easy to see the insanity of these messages if our eyes and ears are attuned to God. Even as in Jeremiah's day, the people who persist in error are those who have their eyes closed and their ears shut to the truth.

How can we think so highly of one human who erred that we kill another in order to relieve the first from the consequence of their mistake? I don't know. That's why I am against abortion. In today's economic mess, the same doctrine is being applied to debt. We are told we must willingly pay the debt for another person who was foolish with his money, using ours that was earned by hard work so the one who was foolish will not suffer overmuch. This is propaganda. It is also becoming the law of the land in the United States.

How do we know if we are experiencing the blessing of a right relationship with God? The symbol of the Holy Spirit is fire. The progressive relationship we have with God is frequently described as a "consuming fire" or a "refining fire."

*The difference between God as a consuming fire and natural fire is just this, that the further you get away from God the more fiercely you feel His burnings, but when you are close to Him, you will find it (the fire) a glorious protection.*

Oswald Chambers

As we train and build relationship with our horse the same is true. One of the first lessons we teach our horse is that safety and security is found near us. Pressure is removed when the horse is close to us, yet respectful of our personal space. As the horse leaves our side and then returns, he begins to understand that pressure and predicament occur when he chooses to leave without our specific direction. Once the horse returns, it finds glorious protection.

Relationships that are not progressive are regressive. There is no such thing as a static relationship between living things. The trainer can never reach a desired level of relationship with her horse, rest on her laurels, and expect the relationship to continue at that same level. The moment a lesson is learned or a new height of relationship achieved, the process of maintenance begins. Unless the relationship continues to progress, to build upon the foundation already built, the connection will begin to deteriorate. Maintenance is necessary for the lessons, concepts, and skills we do not specifically practice in each days learning experience.

Perhaps you worked for weeks and months to build a relationship with your horse and in the process taught your horse to bow. Excellent. Having this success, you decide to move on to another skill to master as you continue to build a relationship with your horse. You become fascinated with a particular area of competition. As you learn the method of teaching the basics of the new event and build confidence that you and your horse can be successful in competing in the new event, you stop practicing the bow. After all, your horse has completely mastered that trick.

As you focus on other lessons and skills, your horse's ability to perform the perfect bow on cue will begin to gradually erode. One day you may be at an event and want to demonstrate to a new friend how well your horse bows. You give the cue and...nothing happens. Without regular maintenance, every skill will get rusty until it eventually disappears. A refresher course will get your horse bowing again, and you learn you have to add the maintenance of desired skills to your training calendar.

Our relationship with God is either progressing—deepening in commitment and shared experience—or it is regressing. Even routine maintenance will not keep this relationship shiny. Only a progressive relationship with God brings vitality, security, peace, joy, and new levels of spiritual insight. Only when we are nearest to God do we enjoy His glorious protection.

Trainers sometimes reach a level of relationship with a horse that they find satisfactory, but when another horse comes along with seemingly greater promise, the first is turned out to pasture. The retired horse will receive excellent care, green pasture, and clean water. It will want for nothing, except a relationship with the trainer. Perhaps there will be other horses in the pasture for company, but what made that horse special has been removed.

Christians can be saved, yet find themselves turned out to pasture as well. If we do not continue building a relationship with God and expand the place where His fire protects us, we may find ourselves locked out of the barn. Yes, we will be saved, but we have lost the special place we might have had if we had continued in a progressive relationship with the Lord.

Progress is only made, whether man or horse, by continuing obedience. Are you progressing in your relationship to the Lord, or are you content to slip away from that relationship? Anyone who tells you that the moment you are saved is the end of the journey is working for the other side. Once you recognize a need for a relationship with Jesus Christ, you have only established a beginning.

# ABANDONMENT

*The Lord is the strength of my life; of whom shall I be afraid?*

Psalm 27:1

*God has great things in store for His people; they ought to have large expectations.*

C.H. Spurgeon

Are you ready to let God lead you into full union with Him, abandoning your right to yourself and becoming fully obedient to His direction? Are you ready to let go of the strings you've been clutching ever more tightly in a desperate attempt to keep the balloons filled with your dreams from floating away? When you abandon to God, you stop asking questions. You trust Him. As soon as you fling off independence you are immediately given freedom unlike anything you ever dreamed of. You will then own the elusive joy and peace you've heard about for years but never understood.

You are not lost in abandonment; you are found. There isn't any maybe or if; you know whether or not you are in a right relationship with God. Not a perfect relationship, but a right relationship. If you are not, it is because you are withholding either obedience or trust from the Lord.

Why is it we think that we will never experience all the possibilities available in the world or escape our parochial little lives unless we make a list of goals for ourselves apart from God? We insist on defining our experience in earthly terms because we do not trust God to handle our affairs or our future; we get independent and pushy. When we do, the unintended result is to stultify our options, to put a governor on our throttle. We limit ourselves by putting a limit on what we allow God to do with us. The only way to remove the ceiling from what is possible and to discover options we never dreamed of is to abandon to God.

It has been said that the journey of a thousand miles begins with a single step. Without a specific destination in mind, we errantly believe we cannot take even the first step. If I have no idea where I am going, should my first step be to the north, south, east, or west? If you feel the need to move from the spot you find yourself rooted to, just take a step. Pick any direction. When Jesus performed healing miracles, He didn't just wave a hand. Jesus required action from the one about to be healed. Jesus would say, "Stretch out your hand," or, "Arise and take up your bed." Jesus never lowered Himself to the sinners' level; He asked sinners to raise themselves to where He was and then to "sin no more."

By focusing on the Lord, you will slowly begin to see where your next step should be, then another, and so on. You will never get anywhere else if you don't go somewhere *else*. In order to change something, you have to change *something*. These are obvious concepts, yet we forget that we know them in the confusion and complexities we create in our lives.

It is a fact that you cannot train a horse without movement. You cannot teach a horse to turn left unless he is moving forward. You cannot teach a horse to "whoa" unless it is already in motion. Highly trained horses often move in a highly collected frame. This means that they are expending greater energy and performing more difficult maneuvers but using that energy to specifically control their muscles rather than increasing speed.

Doesn't it seem counterintuitive to apply more gas to go more slowly? In essence, that is the product of collection in a horse. Highly collected movements have a very high degree of difficulty. Proper training includes conditioning the mind as well as the body. Muscles must be strengthened over time and through repetition before a horse can maintain a collected frame for extended periods of time. It is a highly advanced horse that can make such exertion look so easy. There is a similar training program that Christians go through, learning over time to perform in ever-closer unity with God, where the greatest works look like the least.

**Limitless Vision**

If the highest achievement we can envision with our horse is to be able to ride safely on a familiar trail then that will be the extent to which we will ever be able to enjoy our horse. When we pursue a relationship with our horse with specific goals in mind and a dedication to providing trustworthy and wise leadership, we enable our horse to rise above the restrictions of its prey nature.

There will be times when the blossoming relationship between you and your horse gives you new understanding of your role as a child of God. At other times the Holy Spirit may reveal a biblical truth to you that solves the nagging problem you have been fruitlessly trying to work out with your horse—or your child. Humans expand a horse's ability to achieve greater levels of performance than what would naturally be possible, just as God expands ours. Only in abandonment do our eyes begin to see light where only darkness existed before.

No one has ever found a limit to what the horse-human partnership can accomplish. Most of us lose our way by concentrating on the goal of task and not the depth of relationship. We narrow our focus and get caught seeing only with tunnel vision. Are focus and commitment required to achieve goals? Absolutely. The issue is what we focus on and what goals we set. My point is that we set unnecessary limits on the possible when we establish our focus and goals using only our own intellect and vision. God's vision is limitless.

Abandonment to God opens up delights, emotions, experiences, and insights not possible by any other means. What is a double blessing is that we receive all these benefits married to a deep security of personal safety as we shelter in the shadow of His wing or are lifted above any danger by resting in the palm of His hand. We learn to trust with the simplicity of a child. Is a four-year-old child concerned and depressed because the Russians are presenting a more aggressive military posture? No. That child is unconcerned about those big issues; indeed, she can't even understand the scope of them because mom and dad take care of all that stuff. Most big issues don't even register to a child. Scripture instructs us to be like little children. We are to abandon our cares and concerns to the Lord. Little children are expected to play fair, to share, and to pick up their toys. Responsibility is appropriate to their position and maturity. When it comes to our relationship with God, it is no different; the expectations and responsibilities just look a little different.

Let's examine this concept from the trainer-horse perspective. What does abandonment look like in this relationship? The horse who abandons to the trainer asks no more "why" questions. The relationship the trainer has created with the horse firmly establishes the habit of obedience. Horses love routine and are concerned mainly about food, water, shelter, rest, and relationship with herd mates. Horses play and are inquisitive. Some horses have a low boredom threshold; some are stodgy and a bit obtuse, but all horses must have a leader in order to feel secure. Are we as humans really much different?

When a horse enters training, it has no idea of the possibilities that lie ahead. The trainer knows the plan basics, but the horse must work through each successive lesson and step before each new possibility is presented. Exposing a horse to a concept too far above its experience will result in failure, perhaps injury, and may forever ruin the horse's chance of eventually mastering the concept. Such outcomes are the result of a failure of leadership. People react in much the same way.

As our horse becomes obedient in the small things, we find they are now safe and secure on a simple neighborhood trail ride. Any issues that arise are handled through additional training and by building sturdier foundations. As a new level of performance and trust is built, we can take our horse to a local horse show to compete in a novice rail class and maybe a walk-jog trail class. If we perform well, testing the obedience and concentration of our horse, we either succeed or identify those areas that still need attention. We do not measure the success of our horse by the judge's opinion of our performance, but by the obedience, the abandonment, of our horse to our direction. Most of you probably know what happens when a horse decides it wants a democratic relationship; insisting on a vote before engaging in an

AMAZING GRAYS, AMAZING GRACE

activity or maneuver. My horses and I are a team, but there is no confusion about who leads the team.

There will, however, be instances where I ask the horse to step up and make independent decisions. Without allowing our horses to practice leading they will never develop confidence in their ability to do all the things we want to enjoy with them. Confidence is important. Successful experience builds confidence. Self-confidence allows us to take risks. The greater our confidence, the greater the risks we are willing to take. The more confidence my horse has in me and in "us," the more willing he will be to step out and perform a maneuver he considers risky. In obedience and confidence he will try. Avoiding problems does not develop confidence; facing and resolving problems develops confidence.

As the horse and trainer work through the stages leading to complete abandonment, possibilities explode. The horse that once was afraid to get into a horse trailer or jump over a fallen log can become the horse that competes in the Olympic Games in a distant country.

Do you really think humans are more limited in possibilities than horses? As we abandon more to God, what is possible for us explodes. A ship that never breaks its connection to the pier will never begin a voyage, much less complete one. We will never fully explore what is possible and soar to greater heights if we are not willing to release the strings that tether us to the limits of our own narrow vision.

I particularly love the illustration of abandonment in this verse from Guillaume Appollinaire, a turn-of-the-century Polish poet and philosopher:

*"Come to the edge."*
*"We can't. We're afraid."*
*"Come to the edge."*
*"We can't. We will fall."*
*"Come to the edge."*
*And they came.*
*And he pushed them.*
*And they flew.*

Only in abandonment to God are we certain never to be abandoned. Are you abandoned to God?

# RAPTURE AND TRIBULATION

*And God will wipe away every tear from their eyes; there shall be no more death, nor sorrow, nor crying. There shall be no more pain, for the former things have passed away.*

Revelation 21:4

*The real meaning of eternal life is a life that can face anything it has to face without wavering.*

Oswald Chambers

A centuries-long debate regarding the rapture of Christians and the coming tribulation continues to this day. Have you ever wondered if you will be one of the chosen to be raptured to escape the horrors described in Revelation? Do you believe in a pre-tribulation rapture or a post-tribulation rapture, or one that occurs at the three-and-a-half-year midline of the tribulation? Not too long ago I subscribed to the pre-tribulation timing of the rapture, probably because it was the outcome most comfortable for me to contemplate. All the bad stuff wouldn't happen until I was called home in the "twinkling of an eye"; I would not have to endure the difficulties and atrocities ahead. But if I am to be honest, there was still a nagging voice in my head that asked, "What if I am wrong?" The scholars who teach each of the concepts seem pretty firm in their beliefs and use Scripture to support their various positions. How was I to know for sure if I was right?

Well, I am both blessed and relieved to say that, for me, the issue has finally been put to rest. There is no longer any question in my mind or spirit about the issue of rapture and tribulation. I have peace. My concerns were resolved when I finally understood what the basic question really was. The issue is not when we will be raptured; the issue is our relationship to Jesus Christ.

The book of Revelation to me is indeed the Word of God, divinely inspired, and John accurately spells out the events and conditions of the end of times and the coming Messianic era. All the answers to our questions are contained in the book. However, I also believe that we are not capable of understanding it in our present form. God started the Bible with the beginning, and how else could it properly conclude but at the end? Just as no one knows all there is to know about horses, no one truly understands the entire book of Revelation. Our Teacher may reveal insights about different parts of it to us in our study, but no human will ever gain understanding of the whole.

What changed my viewpoint? How was the issue resolved for me? By realizing that the very act of questioning was an error in and of itself. Worrying about the end of times violates our calling to abandon ourselves to relationship with Jesus Christ. To question and worry proves that we have not yet committed all our trust and all that we have to Him. The only responsibility we have on this earth is to be in a right relationship with Jesus Christ. All other topics are merely subheadings, and our concentration on them is evidence of our distraction, our lack of absolute commitment and failure to focus on our leader. Jesus Christ paid the final bill on Calvary. There is no debate about His faithfulness. Christians in a right relationship with Him will not be sacrificed and our relationship will be carefully maintained on His part until we move into the final home prepared especially for us. Problems in this relationship only occur when we get independent or distracted.

Distraction is a hurdle that I have been required to face time and time again. It will not go away unless I master it someday and move into a maintenance mode. The concept of distraction came to mind today, and by placing myself in the role of the horse, I was able to gain understanding of how I had been in error regarding the end times issue.

When I work with Bo and Swizzle I expect their full and complete attention. There are times when an unusual noise beyond a line of trees or a new object is encountered and their focus on me changes to concentration on the noise or object. Their heads go up, their bodies stiffen, and I know I have lost our connection. For the moment they may even forget I am there. As the leader I understand what happened and immediately and gently ask for them to refocus on me, to ignore everything else, to soften to my hand or leg, and return to relationship. I remind them that they are safe with me, that I have proven myself worthy of their trust, and to follow my direction again.

Worthy horse trainers do not introduce their horses to new objects and surroundings in order to desensitize the horse to those specific things, but to build their confidence that in any situation, and in any surrounding, the horse will feel safe in the relationship. This is the method we use to radically alter the nature of the horse. It would be impossible to desensitize a horse to every possibility and then maintain that state. By experience our horses learn that safety and security come from confidently following our leadership. We build foundation and structure in the relationship for just such occasions. My horses need never ask why; indeed, doing so implies a lack of trust and commitment.

What would it look like to Bo and Swizzle if the events of the tribulation were to occur? If there truly is a pre-tribulation rapture this is a moot point. I won't be here to experience it and the Father will care for them. He cares for every sparrow. I know from experience that He will care for my grays.

In the event that Bo and Swizzle lose their comfortable barn I will be sure to provide shelter for them. They won't care if it is a cave or a palace. As long as our relationship holds and they are safe architecture won't matter. Bo and Swizzle will not worry about a change in accommodations. Jesus Christ was born in a stable, or cave, depending on your belief. How could Bo and Swizzle object to more basic housing? Even if we lose our shelter completely it won't matter. Horses have long lived in areas where there is absolutely no cover and they did quite well. What if our supply of hay and grain disappears because I won't wear the mark of the beast and cannot buy or sell? It will be my responsibility to find water and grazing for Bo and Swizzle. We may need to relocate, but I can ride either one and pony the other as we move together. Need I remind anyone that I will not be abandoned either? Jesus Christ will no more allow me to be cast away without provision than I will Bo and Swizzle. I will follow His lead, and my grays will come along with me.

As parents, will you allow your young children to be concerned about where their next meal comes from or where they will lay their head each night? If they have such concerns, then you have absolutely failed them as parents. This is evidence they do not trust you with their circumstances. Children come into each family believing their parents are faultless. Only when we prove unworthy do our kids learn that we are only human. Before this occurs (and it will occur) we need to have introduced them to Jesus Christ so they may begin to build a relationship with Him.

Do you have plans in place for disaster? Are you prepared for a layoff from your job? Have you made plans for escape and direction if you are forced to leave your home in the middle of the night because of fire or flood? Are you taking care of business? You are the parent; you are responsible. Have you built a foundation of relationship with your children so that when distractions occur you are able to recapture their focus and concentration before they stray too far into danger? The good kid who becomes a troubled teen usually does so due to a failure of a relationship with his or her parents.

Do you worry more about your standard of living or your relationship with Jesus Christ? If it is the former, I can understand your predicament. If your main concerns are what *you* want and not what *He* wants, well, you are probably right to worry.

In his song, "Don't ever sell your saddle," Randy Travis wrote my favorite lyric of all time: "Find the Lord before you need Him." There is no better advice I can give you than this. The only sure way to never be abandoned is by abandoning yourself to Jesus Christ.

Jesus assures us in Revelation 3:8, "I have set before you an open door, and no one can shut it." In verse 10 Jesus continues. "Because you have kept my command to persevere (remain in right relationship with Him), I also will keep you from the hour of trial which shall come upon the whole world, to test those who dwell on the earth."

Distraction from my relationship with Jesus Christ caused my questions and insecurity about the whole rapture-tribulation issue. Being rightly related to Jesus Christ, abandoning to Him, removed my questions and eliminated my concern. I know that as long as I am with Him all will be well. My physical circumstances may change. So what? I know that Jesus Christ alone is worthy, and by remaining rightly related to Him the narrow gate to heaven will remain open until I pass through.

# THE SPOTTED WONDER

*God's finger touched him, and he slept.*

Alfred, Lord Tennyson

Yesterday would have been his eighteenth birthday. I was there when he was born, touching him as he took his first breath on earth. I was there, touching his cheek, when he drew his last breath before returning to his Maker. Not being one prone to shed tears, I find they are threatening to pool and spill over, and I'm still writing the first paragraph.

The tears are of failure and waste—two things I never wanted to be guilty of. But there it is. Most of *Amazing Grays, Amazing Grace* deals with the successes and enjoyment attached to my relationship with Bo and Swizzle and how relationships with other horses over the past two decades have helped me to better understand my relationship with God. The story of my Spotted Wonder will end this book and, perhaps, give you hope for the future as you move forward in your relationships with humans, with horses, and with God.

I would not be giving you the whole story if I left out the part where God blessed me with the specific answer to my prayer and I squandered it. I feel profound shame that I didn't understand the consequences of the choices I made so many years ago. Yet, I am equally thankful that while that door is forever closed, I did learn the lesson it provided. God never seems to run out of lessons, and He never runs out of grace.

A couple of years into my horse career we eagerly awaited the birth of the first foal from our own breeding program. After weeks of careful watching, he arrived at two thirty in the morning. My friend Jackie waited in the lawn chair next to mine in the breezeway of our mare motel. She had been present when hundreds of foals entered the world.

As his mother Sugar, strained with each contraction, the miracle began. First came tiny striped hooves, slippered with thick, golden "gelatin" that allows easy passage through the birth canal; and then a tiny head with a brilliant white blaze, the little tongue out and already cupped; brown shoulders; and then the most perfect snow-white blanket and spots that began halfway down the foal's back and finished where the well-muscled haunches met the hind legs. It was a boy, a perfect little stud colt.

It was love at first sight for me. Sugar, who had done this a number of times before, was not as excited. She rolled up onto her chest and just groaned. Over the years I would learn that Sugar was perfectly content to get her foal out and give its care over to the waiting human. Sugar took good care of her foals, but she didn't really want to get too involved until she had gotten some rest and, hopefully, the hot bran mash she came to expect. For Sugar, it was food first, take care of the kid later.

We waited until the colt finally got to his feet, having wallowed about like a water spider until his legs gathered strength and he gained control of them. By the time he was up, I had toweled him dry, stroked his soft coat countless times, and decided he was going to be my horse forever. This was the horse I had always wanted. That special one. He did not disappoint in any way. He was an answer to prayer.

All went well, or so we thought.

One of the most nerve-racking parts of foaling is being sure the foal gets the first milk, the colostrum. Like humans, the first milk is loaded with antibodies to protect the foal as well as closing up the GI tract and helping to pass the meconium. Once a foal is delivered and all appears normal one must wait for the placenta to pass completely and the foal to stand and nurse. Some foals figure out where the milk is and how to get it way before others. This colt was born with his tongue already out, cupped and ready to put his natural suck reflex to work. Before long, he was looking around for a place to put that tongue to good use. Sugar was not impressed. She had a bellyache, but she dutifully cocked a hind leg to make access easier for the foal.

That tongue was all over. First it got covered in hair looking in the wrong place. I cleaned it off. Was this colt an idiot? How long was it going to take him to find the milk? He was a strong colt with straight legs and came with a big personality. But gracious, he was slow finding breakfast. Eventually he got in the right position and worked that tongue all over Sugar's bag. She had plenty of milk and the stimulation of the colt's attempts caused her to start putting milk out all over. Finally, we heard that good suck sound, got under Sugar from the opposite side, and verified that the colt was indeed nursing. Sugar cleaned out well, and it was time for Jackie and me to head in. Dawn was breaking and we were exhilarated but tired.

The first thing I did when I got up was to go out and see my beautiful colt. His head was covered in sticky milk. He had obviously been under Sugar regularly. Into the house for a bucket of warm water and a washcloth I went, came out, and cleaned him up. He loved the attention. I watched to see him get busy in the milk department again. I heard the sucking sounds and then headed to town with Jackie to get feed.

After a celebratory lunch, we got back mid-afternoon. Our first stop, of course, was the nursery. Something didn't seem right. The colt didn't look quite as strong, and Sugar quickly rebuffed his attempts to get into position under her to nurse. Sugar wanted nothing to do with him and drove him away when he came looking for milk. I went in to see him, his head again covered in dried, sticky milk. I checked Sugar's nipples. They had not been nursed on! The sucking sounds were made by his tongue on her bag but not sucking milk. He was dehydrated, and he needed attention. We put a halter on Sugar and tried to get the baby over to nurse. He went, he looked, he sucked, but he just did not know how to get the nipples to work. He just kept that little dry tongue cupped but never got it right.

Our veterinarian came almost immediately. We milked Sugar to get milk for Dr. Madia to tube into the baby. We made sure the colt had adequate fluids and was still strong enough. He was. He always would be. The vet gave instructions to try to get him to nurse regularly and to bottle feed him a few ounces of milk every few hours, if absolutely necessary. Not too much because then the colt might feel satisfied and stop looking. Even given this rocky beginning, the veterinarian asked if he was for sale. I didn't think so, but I asked why the interest so soon. Dr. Madia said that many people wait a lifetime for a colt like mine and never get one. This foal was special. I thought so too.

Once her bag had been milked down, Sugar was much more comfortable but still not too happy with the dumb kid. She figured that if he was too stupid to nurse, he should be my responsibility, not hers. Well, that was not an acceptable response, so Jackie and I took turns trying to teach the colt remedial nursing. First, she would hold Sugar and require her to stand quietly, even if not patiently, while I tried to guide the baby's tongue to the right place. When I failed, we changed places. He always got there but just didn't get the suck thing right.

Getting out the nipple and bottle the vet had left, I milked Sugar into a yellow, plastic, four-cup mixing bowl and poured the thick, sticky milk into the soft, plastic bottle. If you have never milked a mare, let me tell you it is not easy. You strip each nipple just like a cow, but the nipple is usually about one-inch long and the milk only comes out with a gentle pull. We have a vet now who has perfected a method of milking a mare more quickly, but we didn't know how to do that all those years ago. I found that warm, wet fingers work the best to milk a mare. I used that same yellow mixing bowl and bottle many times over the next twenty years.

Once I had two or three ounces of milk in the bottle, I attached the lamb nipple and went over to the colt. He knew the smell of milk and was interested right away. I wiggled one finger in the corner of his mouth to open it. Of course, that little tongue was still out and cupped. I lay the nipple in the curl of his tongue, tilted his head up, and let a few drops of milk slide into his mouth. Then I let a few more drops dribble in. The colt shook his head out of my hand, swallowed, and then came looking for more. I put the nipple back into the curl of his tongue; he laid his tongue around the nipple, made a solid connection, and...sucked! He swallowed the entire bottle in about two seconds. We have suck!

The first swallow of warm milk was what the poor baby had been working for since his tongue first made connection with air. He was born with his tongue sticking out in suck position, and he had finally gotten the job done. He wanted more! Of course, he figured I was the source of the milk, and he just followed me around the pen asking for more. It was time to put Sugar back into the equation. Jackie and I set up again, she holding Sugar and me trying to get the now motivated colt into nursing position. I used the milky nipple to lead his nose to Sugar's udder.

This story could go on forever, but let's just say that when I finally got his tongue on the nipple, the connection was made and nature took over. After one more warm head-washing to get the milk off his face and a few more sessions with Sugar, the saga came to a wonderful end and we never had another medical issue with this colt again that wasn't directly caused by a human.

How close we had come to losing this first foal. I never, ever again took any chances on whether or not a new foal nursed correctly. My general rule was to give babies about an hour to figure out how to nurse and then milked mama and bottle-fed the baby their first course when necessary. There were foals I had to bottle feed (or even syringe feed) for quite a while until they were strong enough or coordinated enough to nurse on their own.

We named this beautiful colt Abduls Bright Sky, "Sky" for short. It was interesting, though annoying, that many of the colts he sired were also a bit backward about nursing like their daddy. His fillies were smarter. Isn't nature interesting?

Sky had the most engaging personality. He loved people, even kids. Sky was smart. Sky was gorgeous. Sky was a miracle for me. He was the answer to my prayer. He was to be my horse. Whatever I expected of him, he was always more.

Time passed. Sky was weaned and was given his own stall and pen. He learned manners; he learned everything I tried to teach him. He was nearly perfect. Perfect color, head, legs, muscling, disposition, pedigree, conformation, everything. Sky was born to be a stallion. Wasn't I the luckiest woman in the world?

*Before Sky became The Spotted Wonder*

Sky started his show career before he was twelve months old. He was mature for his age and a real head-turner; tiny ears, square muzzle, shallow mouth, huge hip, and that color. Both his parents had been extremely successful in the show pen. Over the next five years, Sky would follow in their hoof steps with equal success.

Sky was a halter champion, having earned his Register of Merit before he was eighteen months old. As a yearling, he was the high point halter stallion of all ages for our region. Sky was collecting wins; I was learning how to condition and show a halter horse. He was also beginning to exhibit a bit more opinion than I was always prepared for. Yet his disposition remained kind. Sky was beginning to require more leadership in order to get him to go along with my program. Yet he did go along.

Sky was twenty months old when I started him under saddle. It was late December of his yearling year. At the time, I didn't do much preparatory groundwork. I pretty much just saddled and went forward with young horses. After only four times wearing a saddle, four times with a bit in his mouth, and four rides under our belts, Sky would walk on command, jog, side-pass, open and close gates and back. After only four rides! The sixth time I ever saddled him, we delivered Christmas gifts to our neighbors. I wore a backpack loaded with gifts and rode Sky. We played Santa together. He was amazing. I had an equine prodigy on my hands.

Less than two weeks into our riding career, Sky and I walked out the front gate of our property onto the gravel road. We hadn't gotten too far when a huge, yellow backhoe rounded a corner not far away and rumbled directly toward us. What in the world would I do? Would Sky spook and run into the street? Buck? Having no other option, I sat as calmly as I possibly could and waited to see if Sky and I would survive this calamity. Had I made a potentially fatal mistake by riding this absolutely green colt out onto the road?

What happened? Nothing. Sky could not have cared less. His ego was certainly not fragile enough to be concerned about that loud, dusty, stinky machine. Sky's legend was already building in my mind. Perhaps that was the day I truly started going down the wrong path. Or maybe it was a day or two later when Sky and I were trekking through the high Sonoran desert just north of our property. We were on a trail that came upon a large Saguaro cactus. The path we were on went within six feet of the giant cactus. Just before we got to the twenty-foot-high, multi-armed Saguaro, Sky abruptly stopped. *Why*, I wondered, *did he stop?*

Sky was absolutely calm. He looked directly at the cactus, his nose about two feet off the ground in its normal traveling position. Sky didn't move his body at all except to begin to slowly raise his head, examining the cactus from where it started at ground level until his nose was pointed skyward, his eyes reaching the very top of the cactus. Having satisfied his curiosity, Sky slowly lowered his head and neck back to normal traveling position and quietly began walking along the path again. If there had been any question before, I was now absolutely convinced that Sky was special. I was right.

Sky was such a special gift from God. Had I only recognized it and accepted it with gratitude and humility, this story would end much differently. However, I did not.

My failure was one of relationship. I thought I was ready to be his leader. I was not. I determined that Sky was to be my horse…my partner forever. Indeed, he could have been. He was prepared to do his part but I was too ignorant and arrogant to do mine. We had great success but there was always a part of him I didn't have. Sky would have given it, but I didn't know how to ask for it, to earn it, or to deserve it.

I wanted to win. I wanted to begin making a name for both our horse program and myself. I sacrificed what I had prayed for - a perfect equine partner. God gave him to me. I wasted the chance. Foolishly, I started Sky's breeding career as a two-year-old, before he had time to fully learn to be a performance horse.

Sky still became a champion. As a weanling. As a yearling. A star pupil when I started him under saddle. A National and World champion reining horse. Sky sired champions. At his first World Show under saddle he tied for Reserve World Champion All-Around Western horse.

Sky excelled at all he did yet he was difficult in some ways. He was always a stallion first and a show horse second. His ground manners were good, but he would periodically challenge riders to test their leadership ability.

The little hints that our relationship was not as it should be kept coming but I didn't see them for what they were. Sky wouldn't lunge without a chain even as a new yearling—perfect evidence of a hole in the foundation of our relationship. John Lyons personally worked on the lunging issue but was not able to make the connection with Sky. It was the beginning of the break that would keep us from being rightly related and limit the extent to which both he and I would go. By the time I finally began to go back to repair our foundation, time was quickly running out.

Sky never had a mean hair on him. You could have put a toddler in his stall without concern. Sky would either step around them or nuzzle them. He challenged authority on occasion, but if he found the human wanting he simply left the scene. He never tried to bite, kick, or strike. He just dismissed the person and tried to leave them behind. My worst mistake was yet to come.

My husband and I moved to Texas in 1999 to concentrate on breeding quarter horses for reining and cutting. Sky, of course, came along as "my horse." I started doing reining maneuvers with him again and wanted to be sure he was still good enough for open NRHA (National Reining Horse Association) competition. Upon the advice of a trusted advisor, I took Sky to a trainer I did not personally know to get checked out. Rather than work through the process with Sky myself, I took the easy way out. After all, I was building a new facility and working on the new program. It was an easy choice for me; disastrous for Sky.

Within a few months, Sky was home again, injured, and forever changed. Sky had never been mean. He still wasn't. Even worse, Sky had learned fear. Most horses choose to run when they are afraid. Sky had learned to attack before he was attacked. He was only home a few days when he came at me teeth first as I entered his stall with the cleaning cart. There was fear in his eyes. I'll never know exactly what happened to him, but Sky would never be the same again.

Over time Sky learned to pretty much trust me again. This trust did not extend to my husband or anyone else, and it was no longer a pure trust. Sky was gelded, and we tried to figure out what his physical problem was. Great veterinarians worked on him but didn't nail down the problem for a long time. I turned him out to pasture for a year. That was hard on a horse that was raised as a pampered champion with bedded stall and blankets. Sky hated the pasture, but I hoped the time off would repair whatever was wrong.

Eventually we figured it out, did surgery, and Sky was sound again. We were never able to return his complete confidence, and he could be difficult in the barn and under saddle. The truth was, I loved Sky, but he was a pain to deal with at times. My husband and he did not get along, and he was not reliable. Wow, that was a hard one to live with. I had failed him miserably. Our program had no place for a spotted wonder anymore. He was difficult. I had a full barn. Sky went out to pasture again.

About a year later, I realized that Sky would just get old if he simply stayed out in the pasture. I brought him back into the barn and started riding him again. My leadership and training skills had improved greatly in the intervening couple of years, and I had new skills to use with Sky. They worked. Sky was behaving well, both under saddle and in the barn. He and my husband still weren't friends, but they could coexist. I called Terry Thompson, a trainer who had known Sky nearly his whole life and who had done really well with one of Sky's daughters. He was ready to try Sky out for a client, knowing the condition I set that Sky would have to stay in his barn and under his control as long as he was away from home. I trusted Terry. He lived up to both Sky's expectations and mine. Sky knew how to do most anything. He was important again. He was a show horse again. All went well for nearly a year.

One day Terry called and said that Sky was getting nervous at shows and becoming too difficult for a non-pro to handle. I said I would be right up to get him and bring him home. Truthfully, I missed him and was happy to be able to have him in the barn again. Still amazingly beautiful, it seemed Sky and I might finally have our time together.

Sky hadn't been back more than a few days, and delightful days they had been, when I realized there was a problem. I went into his stall to clean. He was perfectly calm, happy to have me there, and promptly ran his head into the handle of the cleaning fork. Sky was blind in one eye. No wonder he had become nervous in strange surroundings. He could not see at all out of his left eye.

The first glimmer of returning fear started to appear. Sky was absolutely sweet except when he was startled. We worked on trust issues, but it is difficult when you can't train one side of his brain. Still, we got along pretty well, and while I knew our show career was over, I hoped we could still develop the relationship we were meant to have.

The reality of the coming downturn in the horse market was swiftly becoming apparent. I worked as an equine consultant and appraiser, so I had a good handle on the facts. We started selling our broodmares in 2005 and then sold the ranch as well. Originally we hoped to keep two really good broodmares, but the market just kept going down and we eventually sold out completely.

We built a house and small barn on a hay field a mile from the old place. Sky moved with us and took up residence in one of the four brand new stalls. I was prepared to treat him like the champion he was and continue to work on our relationship. Within a few months, I noticed Sky kick out with both hind feet at nothing. He was in his stall and there wasn't even a horse next to him at the time. It appeared he thought something had moved and he had reverted to fight first and ask questions later. It happened again. Sky was also losing the sight in his right eye. Fear was causing problems again. This time, though, I was out of options. Sky wasn't safe in the barn anymore. He could hurt himself and might possibly hurt my husband without meaning to. Sky was put out to pasture once again. His pasture mates were a young donkey and a retired broodmare who was very passive.

Sky became the boss of the little herd, and the trio became a contented little group. Over the next few months, however, the donkey began to give Sky less and less respect. As his remaining eyesight failed, Sky began to depend on the old mare to lead him around. Still, he was happy. Sky was content. He somehow forgot fear as he became abandoned to dependency. I loved to go to the pasture, hug and pet on him, and spend time as we had when he was a new foal. He followed me, just as he had when I was teaching him to nurse that first morning so many years ago.

Sky was still absolutely gorgeous. Sky was sweet again. God blessed us both by giving him a handicap that removed his fear and replaced it with sweet trust in me again. Our veterinarian examined his eyes and told us he had little, if any, sight remaining. Still, he seemed to get along well in his now-familiar pasture. The mare was nearing thirty years old, and we knew that Sky would only have as much time as she did. He would never be able to get along without her.

Why was I surprised that things did not work out as planned with Sky? God was at work again. We planned on leaving for Arizona the next week. It was July; it was hot. I looked out to the pasture a few days before we were to leave and noticed the mare and donkey drinking, but not Sky. He had been having more and more difficulty finding the feeder each day. He seemed afraid to put his head into the open trough but would if we coaxed him to it. *Perhaps*, I thought, *he's already had a drink and all is well*. The mare walked off, and Sky stayed near the waterer but did not drink. Eventually he moved off to follow the mare.

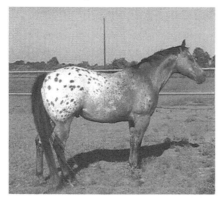

*The last photo of Sky.*

The same thing happened later that day. I went out to put a halter on Sky and led him to the waterer to see if he was thirsty. I fully expected Sky to go with me but not drink. I was wrong again. Sky followed me trustingly, and when I had his nose near the water, he dove in and drank long and deep. It was obvious that something had changed. I don't know what. Sky was not able to get water by himself just as he was not able to get to his feed by himself. Sky would follow me in the open but would not go under the shade.

How grateful I was to notice that Sky wasn't drinking before we left for Arizona. He was spared what might have been a torturous end. This time I did not fail him. I called the vet. I let Sky go. Just as I had been with him at his first breath, I stroked his beautiful head until he drew his last breath. At long last I was worthy of the trust he placed in me.

I had failed as Sky's leader. I failed to appreciate the answer to my prayer. I had been arrogant. God does not give us open-ended opportunities. When God closes a door it stays closed forever. However, He is faithful to open another and offer us yet another chance to learn the lesson He has for us.

Is it a coincidence that I am writing this on Good Friday? I think not.

I am guilty.

I am ashamed.

I had not done right by Sky. The Lord picked up where I could not go and took care of Sky at the end. It was a blessing for such a noble animal to not have to live another decade or more, blind, in the pasture. Sky was not born to that life. He was born to a relationship with me. I blew it. God was faithful to Sky even when I wasn't. I missed the signs.

God had offered me the exact relationship I had wanted since I was four years old. He gave me just what I asked for. I didn't recognize it. I wasn't ready. Arrogance and pride got in the way.

God, the Father, provided Jesus Christ, His Son, so each of us would have the opportunity to enjoy the exact relationship we all need. We are all guilty. Only when we feel the burning shame that drives us to our knees can we enter into a right relationship with Jesus Christ.

Jesus hung on the cross for me. He hung there for you. Do not miss the greatest gift the Father has ever given. Jesus Christ is there for you, but you must give up your arrogance and pride in order to receive what you truly desire. Don't make the same mistake I did. Sky was not my only failure. There will always be another lesson, another door. But by the grace of God, the sacrifice of His Son, and the tutelage of His Spirit, I have peace, I have joy, and I am saved.

Through the miracle of His grace, I was given another chance. My work of the past thirty-five years has come together in the leadership work I do with people and with my amazing grays. Would it surprise you if I told you no one besides me has ever ridden Bo? That may change someday, but in the meantime, I will not fail him.

I am forever changed by God's amazing grace.

# ACKNOWLEDGMENTS

Thank you to each of the very special people and horses who have blessed my life, without whom there would be no *Amazing Grays, Amazing Grace*. For those who have already passed through the Narrow Gate, I'll meet you on the other side one day soon.

Above all, I am grateful to be a chosen child of God, blessed by the Holy Spirit with the scent of freedom.

## UPDATE:

God wastes nothing. The three years between the first and second editions of *Amazing Grays* were filled with more lessons, opportunities, and adventures as well as two new books.

During that time our foundational messages of faith that overcomes fear through worthy leadership have been simplified in some respects, expanded in others. I am still in training and look forward to each new day lived with horses and Jesus Christ. My husband and I now live in the barn with four dogs, three cats, my beloved amazing grays, two of Sky's sons who returned home in a way only God could engineer (read their story in *He Came Looking for Me*), and Copper and Asti.

We pray for every person reached through the ministry each day. May you be richly blessed by right relationship with God, horses, and the special people dearest to your own heart.

I'll be looking for you at the Gate!  -  Lynn

# ABOUT THE AUTHOR

A former business consultant and motivational speaker, Christian writer Lynn Baber exchanged the board room for the barn at the end of the 1980's. Her success as an equine professional includes achievement as a World and National Champion horse breeder and trainer, judge, Certified Equine Appraiser, and expert witness.

The primary message of Lynn's work is "Faith over Fear." She openly shares lessons learned from personal experience with domestic violence, hopelessness, serious family illness, failure, perseverance, and success. Lynn teaches the principles of being a worthy leader and the pursuit of true fearlessness in today's world.

Lynn says the messages she delivered as a motivational speaker were absolutely correct, but today she knows where these principles are found in the Bible. Whether shared in print, in person, or in the round pen working with troubled horses, the message will always be God's faithfulness and grace.

Living her dream in Weatherford, Texas, Lynn and her husband Baber (Larry) share the barn with their horses, dogs, cats and goats. She says, "It took me more than three decades of success to finally live in the barn."

Other titles by Lynn Baber:

***Rapture and Revelation*** - Welcome to the End Time, (2012)

*The King is coming. This is the End Time and a choice must be made between God and Not God. Why do you believe what you believe? Many Christians have been shocked to discover that the "jesus" they know is not the Son of God. Simple, direct, and includes citations of the scriptures that support the message.*

***He Came Looking for Me*** - A true story of hope and redemption, (2011)

*What do the story of an unwanted horse and the promise of a mansion in heaven have in common? Destined for the slaughterhouse, Shiner, shares his story with readers proving that no matter how hopeless your circumstances appear, God's promises are true. The amazing grays are back again as life in the barn continues. If you loved "Black Beauty" don't miss Shiner's story. Includes a Discussion Section for book or study groups.*

***The Art of Being Foolish Proof***: the best kept customer service secret, (1989)

Contact information:

PO Box 187, Weatherford, TX 76086

www.AmazingGraysMinistry.com

lynn@amazinggraysministry.com

14702034R00175

Made in the USA
San Bernardino, CA
03 September 2014